A Field Guide to
MELANCHOLY

Jacky Bowring

OLDCASTLE BOOKS

This edition published in 2015
First published in 2008 by Oldcastle Books,
PO Box 394, Harpenden, Herts,
AL5 1XJ, UK

oldcastlebooks.co.uk

A CIP catalogue record for this book is available from the
British Library.

ISBN
978-1-84344-623-1 (print)
978-1-84344-611-8 (epub)
978-1-84344-612-5 (kindle)
978-1-84344-613-2 (pdf)

2 4 6 8 10 9 7 5 3

Typeset by Avocet Typeset, Somerton, Somerset, TA11 6RT

Printed in Great Britain by 4edge Limited, Essex

For Jasper and Ella

Rosalind: They say you are a melancholy fellow.
Jaques: I am so; I do love it better than laughing.

Shakespeare, *As You Like It*

Contents

Introduction

Laurence Aberhart, *Files, Wanganui, 1 July 1986*

Introduction

Melancholy is a twilight state; suffering melts into it and becomes a sombre joy. Melancholy is the pleasure of being sad.
Victor Hugo, *Toilers of the Sea*[1]

Melancholy is ambivalent and contradictory. Although it seems at once a very familiar term, it is extraordinarily elusive and enigmatic. It is something found not only in humans – whether pathological, psychological, or a mere passing mood – but in landscapes, seasons, and sounds. They too can be melancholy. Batman, Pierrot, and Hamlet are all melancholic characters, with traits like darkness, unrequited longing, and genius or heroism. Twilight, autumn and minor chords are also melancholy, evoking poignancy and the passing of time.

How is melancholy defined? *A Field Guide to Melancholy* traces out some of the historic traditions of melancholy, most of which remain today, revealing it to be an incredibly complex term. Samuel Johnson's definition, in his eighteenth century *Dictionary of the English Language*, reveals melancholy's multi-faceted nature was already well established by then: 'A *disease*, supposed to proceed from a redundance of black bile; a kind of *madness*, in which the mind is always fixed on one object; a gloomy, pensive, discontented *temper.*'[2] All of these aspects – disease, madness and temperament – continue to coalesce in the concept of melancholy, and rather than seeking a definitive definition or chronology, or a discipline-specific account, this book embraces contradiction and paradox: the very kernel of melancholy itself.

As an explicit promotion of the ideal of melancholy, the *Field Guide* extols the benefits of the pursuit of sadness, and questions the obsession with happiness in contemporary society. Rather than seeking an 'architecture of happiness', or resorting to Prozac-with-everything, it is proposed that melancholy is not a negative emotion, which for much of history it wasn't – it was a desirable condition, sought for its 'sweetness' and intensity. It remains an important point of balance – a counter to the 'loss of sadness'. Not grief, not mourning, not sorrow, yet all of those things.

Melancholy is profoundly interdisciplinary, and ranges across fields as diverse as medicine, literature, art, design, psychology and philosophy. It is over two millennia old as a concept, and its development pre-dates the emergence of disciplines. While similarly enduring concepts have also been tackled by a breadth of disciplines such as philosophy, art and literature, melancholy alone extends across the spectrum of arts *and* sciences, with significant discourses in fields like psychiatry, as much as in art. Concepts with such an extensive period of development (the idea of 'beauty' for example) tend to go through a process of metamorphosis and end up meaning something distinctly different.[3] Melancholy has been surprisingly stable. Despite the depth and breadth of investigation, the questions, ideas and contradictions which form the 'constellation'[4] of melancholy today are not dramatically different from those at any time in its history. There is a sense that, as psychoanalytical theorist Julia

Kristeva puts it, melancholy is 'essential and trans-historical'.[5]

Melancholy is a central characteristic of the human condition, and Hildegard of Bingen, the twelfth century abbess and mystic, believed it to have been formed at the moment that Adam sinned in taking the apple – when melancholy 'curdled in his blood'.[6] Modern day Slovenian philosopher, Slavoj Žižek, also positions melancholy, and its concern with loss and longing, at the very heart of the human condition, stating 'melancholy (disappointment with all positive, empirical objects, none of which can satisfy our desire) is in fact the beginning of philosophy.'[7]

The complexity of the idea of melancholy means that it has oscillated between attempts to define it scientifically, and its embodiment within a more poetic ideal. As a very coarse generalisation, the scientific/psychological underpinnings of melancholy dominated the early period, from the late centuries BC when ideas on medicine were being formulated, while in later, mainly post-medieval times, the literary ideal became more significant. In recent decades, the rise of psychiatry has re-emphasised the scientific dimensions of melancholy. It was never a case of either/or, however, and both ideals, along with a multitude of other colourings, have persisted through history.

The essential nature of melancholy as a bodily as well as a purely mental state is grounded in the foundation of ideas on physiology; that it somehow relates to the body itself. These ideas are rooted in the ancient notion of 'humours'. In Greek and Roman times humoralism was the foundation for an understanding of physiology, with the four humours ruling the body's characteristics.

Phlegm, blood, yellow bile and black bile were believed to be the four governing elements, and each was ascribed to particular seasons, elements and temperaments. This can be expressed via a tetrad, or four-cornered diagram.

The four-part divisions of temperament were echoed in a number of ways, as in the work of Alkindus, the ninth century Arab philosopher, who aligned the times of the day with particular dispositions. The tetrad could therefore be further embellished, with the first quarter of the day sanguine, second choleric, third melancholic and

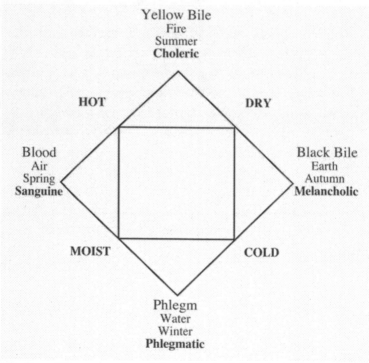

The Four Humours, adapted from Henry E Sigerist (1961) *A History of Medicine*, 2 vols New York: Oxford University Press, 2:232.[8]

finally phlegmatic. Astrological allegiances reinforce the idea of four quadrants, so that Jupiter is sanguine, Mars choleric, Saturn is melancholy, and the moon or Venus is phlegmatic. The organs, too, are associated with the points of the humoric tetrad, with the liver sanguine, the gall bladder choleric, the spleen melancholic, and the brain/lungs phlegmatic.

Melancholy, then, is associated with twilight, autumn, earth, the spleen, coldness and dryness, and the planet Saturn. All of these elements weave in and out of the history of melancholy, appearing in mythology, astrology, medicine, literature and art. The complementary humours and temperaments were sometimes hypothesised as balances, so that the opposite of one might be introduced as a remedy for an excess of another. For melancholy, the introduction of sanguine elements – blood, air and warmth – could counter the darkness. This could also work at an astrological level, as in the appearance of the magic square of Jupiter on the wall behind Albrecht Dürer's iconic engraving *Melencolia I*, (1514) – the sign of Jupiter to introduce a sanguine balance to the saturnine melancholy angel.

In this early phase of the development of humoral thinking a key tension arose, as on one hand it was devised as a means of establishing degrees of wellness, but on the other it was a system of types of disposition. As Klibansky, Panofsky and Saxl put it, there were two quite different meanings to the terms sanguine, choleric, phlegmatic and melancholy, as either 'pathological states or constitutional aptitudes'.[9] Melancholy became far more connected with the idea of illness than the other temperaments, and was considered a 'special problem'.

The blurry boundary between an illness and a mere temperament was a result of the fact that many of the symptoms of 'melancholia' were mental, and thus difficult to objectify, unlike something as apparent as a disfigurement or wound. The theory of the humours morphed into psychology and physiognomy, with particular traits or appearances associated with each temperament.

Melancholy was aligned with 'the lisping, the bald, the stuttering and the hirsute', and 'emotional disturbances' were considered as indicators of 'mental melancholy'.[10] Hippocrates in his *Aphorismata,* or 'Aphorisms,' in 400 BC noted, 'Constant anxiety and depression are signs of melancholy.' Two centuries later the physician Galen, in an uncharacteristically succinct summation, noted that Hippocrates was 'right in summing up all melancholy symptoms in the two following: Fear and Depression.'[11]

The foundations of the ideas on melancholy are fraught with complexity and contradiction, and this signals the beginning of a legacy of richness and debate. We have a love-hate relationship with melancholy, recognising its potential, yet fearing its connotations. What is needed is some kind of guide book, to know how to recognise it, where to find it – akin to the Observer's Guides, the Blue Guides, or Gavin Pretor-Pinney's *The Cloudspotter's Guide.* Yet, to attempt to write a guide to such an amorphous concept as melancholy is overwhelmingly impossible, such is the breadth and depth of the topic, the disciplinary territories, the disputes, and the extensive creative outpourings. There is a tremendous sense of the infinite, like staring at stars, or at a room full of files, a daunting multitude. The approach is, therefore, to adopt the notion of the 'constellation', and to plot various points and co-ordinates, a join-the-dots approach to exploration which roams far and wide, and connects ideas and examples in a way which seeks new combinations and sometimes un-expected juxtapositions.

A Field Guide to Melancholy is therefore in itself a melan-cholic enterprise: for the writer, and the reader, the very idea of a 'field guide' to something so contradictory, so elu-sive, embodies the impossibility and futility that is central to melancholy's yearning. Yet, it is this intangible, potent possibility which creates melancholy's magnetism, recalling Joseph Campbell's version of the Buddhist advice to:

Joyfully participate in the sorrows of the world.[12]

Notes

1. Victor Hugo, *Toilers of the Sea,* vol. 3, p.159.
2. Samuel Johnson, *A Dictionary of the English Language,* p.458, em-phasis mine.
3. This constant shift in the development of concepts is well-illus-trated by Umberto Eco (ed) (2004) *History of Beauty.* New York: Rizzoli, and his recent (2007) *On Ugliness,* New York: Rizzoli.
4. The term 'constellation' is Giorgio Agamben's, and captures the sense of melancholy's persistence as a collection of ideas, rather than one simple definition. See Giorgio Agamben, *Stanzas: Word and Phan-tasm in Western Culture,* p.19.
5. Julia Kristeva, *Black Sun: Depression and Melancholia,* p.258.
6. Raymond Klibansky, Erwin Panofsky and Fritz Saxl, *Saturn and Melancholy: Studies in the History of Natural Philosophy, Religion and Art,* p.79.
7. Slavoj Žižek, *Did Somebody say Totalitarianism? Five Interventions on the (Mis)use of a Notion,* p.148.
8. In Stanley W Jackson (1986), *Melancholia and Depression: From Hip-pocratic Times to Modern Times,* p.9.

9. Raymond Klibansky, Erwin Panofsky and Fritz Saxl, *Saturn and Melancholy: Studies in the History of Natural Philosophy, Religion and Art*, p.12.

10. ibid, p.15.

11. ibid, p.15, and n.42.

12. A phrase used by Campbell in his lectures, for example on the DVD Joseph Campbell (1998) *Sukhavati*. Acacia.

The Conundrums of Melancholy: Madness, Genius and Beauty

Laurence Aberhart, *War memorial #2, Balclutha, 1980*

1

The Conundrums of Melancholy: Madness, Genius and Beauty

Bob: It's a sad and beautiful world.
Zach:Yeah, it's a sad and beautiful world, buddy.
Jim Jarmusch, *Down By Law*[1]

Suffering and joy. Pleasure and sadness. Melancholy is a conundrum, a riddle of contradictions. The latent richness of the concept grows out of these paradoxes, and three particular enigmas haunt melancholy: madness, genius and beauty. Why should being sad mean that you're mad? Why are geniuses and heroes so often melancholy? And, how can things that are sorrowful be beautiful?

Melancholy and Madness: 'A disorder of the intellect'

Madness hangs around melancholy from the beginnings of the idea two and a half millennia ago. The wavering boundary between what might be considered simply a mood, or a disposition, and a more serious disorder has never been resolved. Science's dominion over melancholy as an illness has long sought to clarify the symptoms of insanity. But melancholy has always remained elusive, evading systems of rigid classification, and the situation becomes even more complicated in recent times with 'depression' added to the complex condition.

Early investigations of melancholy were based on humoral theory, and melancholy was simply one amongst four types of humoral imbalance, rather than any exceptional or alarming condition. Historians of medicine point to concerns, even amongst the ancients, about distinguishing mere temperaments from serious disorders. In the diagnosis of a 'melancholic', what was required was the identification of a *disproportionate* expression of sadness, for example in the magnitude or sustained nature of grief, or in wretchedness without a normal cause. This foundational judgment, rooted in the words of Hippocrates ('If fear or sadness last for a long time it is melancholia'), persists to the present day, almost word for word, in the *Diagnostic and Statistical Manual* of the American Psychiatric Association.

These early foundations of the idea hung together as melancholy travelled through time and space. In medieval times in the West it was in the cathedral schools and monasteries that the thinking on melancholia survived, just as many other concepts and aspects of knowledge did. In this religious setting the original ideas became cross-pollinated, and religious misdemeanours and medical explanations were elided in the explanations of melancholy and madness.

The understandings of melancholy that underpinned the Western medical tradition were added to as further information came from the East via translations of the works of, particularly, Middle Eastern scholars like the ninth century Alkindus (Al Kindi) and tenth century Avicenna (Ibn'Sina). The humoral traditions of Galen were continued in this work. The emphasis was on the treatment of humoral imbalances, eliminating the black bile by bathing and other means, for example, and remedies such as coitus were suggested because they 'dissipated fixed ideas of the soul and calmed ungovernable passions'.[2]

The Byzantine Paul of Aegina noted that 'Melancholy is a disorder of the intellect without fever',[3] and he identified a range of symptomatic behaviours of those afflicted, including prophesying, suffering from delusions of being animals, and identifying as an earthen-vessel. This latter delusion is believed to derive from black bile's alliance with 'earth', and occurs also in Arabic writings around this time, as a feeling of being made of clay, which again produces anxiety in the sufferer, and fear of being broken. Foretelling the future had earlier been considered one of the gifts of melancholy, associated with exceptional insight, as with the connection to genius in the following section. At this time though, prophesying was considered another sign of madness.

Later medieval times continued the legacies inherited from the ancients, including the root idea of 'fear and sadness' being out of proportion or without cause, but added to this was the idea of *acedia* – or what is sometimes termed 'sloth'. Monks in particular were afflicted by *acedia*; it was an occupational hazard. Their necessary detachment from the ordinary world of daily activities in order to release them to a life of asceticism and dedication to prayer meant that monks sometimes descended into a state of torpor. This was not only seen as a type of melancholic sickness, but also a deadly sin, persisting today as the sin of Sloth. *Acedia*, and its companion *tristitia*, are outlined in chapter 3, where the *Field Guide* plots a number of the allied terms which enrich ideas on melancholy.

Another spectre of insanity associated with melancholy was witchcraft. Things that were unexplainable, like exceptional memory or prophesying, were beyond what might be considered normal, and placed in the category of insanity. For several centuries this fear and lack of comprehension was explained away as a particular type of madness – witchcraft. This 'mad' melancholy is what Frances Yates called 'bad melancholy', as opposed to the 'good melancholy' of geniuses and heroes. During Elizabethan times, melancholia, madness and witchcraft were closely linked. Satan rather than Saturn became the governing force for melancholy in the eyes of those who considered it a sign of possession by the devil, or a punishment for evil. At this time, the 'mad' version of melancholy was mainly associated with women, who were, in the words of sixteenth century Dutch doctor and 'proto-psychopathologist' Jan Weir: 'raving, poor, simple, useless, ignorant, gullible, stupid, vile, uneducated, infatuated, toothless, silly, unsteady ...old.'[4]

Fears of witchcraft were rife in the colonies, as in the Salem witch trials of the late seventeenth century. Cotton Mather, a Puritan New England minister involved in the trials, sought both religious and pathological explanations for melancholy. Influenced by medical texts and the legacy of humoralism, Mather hedged his bets, and explained melancholy as being related to 'flatulencies in the region of the Hypochondria as well as a degree of diabolical possession'.[5] The reported manifestations of melancholy madness echo those from the Middle Ages, as in the delusions of being 'metamorphosized into a china jar' or 'transformed into a smoking pidgeon pie'.[6]

One of the key texts in the history of the complexities

of melancholy was Robert Burton's massive tome, published in 1621, which bears the title: *The Anatomy of Melancholy, What it is: With all the Kinds, Causes, Symptomes, Prognostickes, and Several Cures of it. In Three Maine Partitions with their several Sections, Members, and Subsections. Philosophically, Historically, Opened and Cut up.*[7] Burton, an Oxford don writing under the pseudonym Democritus Junior, set out to describe all the forms of melancholy, including head melancholy, hypochondriacal melancholy, religious melancholy, love melancholy, and 'Maids, Nuns, and Widows' Melancholy'. This form of definition by description, running to some 783 pages in the first edition, rather than achieving any kind of precision served to further emphasise the complexity of melancholy. The pseudonym of Democritus Junior linked Burton back to the age of Hippocrates, and allowed him a detached perspective from which to construct his work. He told a tale where Hippocrates came across Democritus in his garden at Abdera, sitting with a book on his lap, and 'the subject of his book was melancholy and madness: and around him lay the carkasses of several beasts, newly cut up by him and anatomized; not that he did condemn Gods creatures, as he told Hippocrates, but to find out the seat of this *altra bilis*, or melancholy, whence it proceeds, and how it is engendred into mens bodies, to the intent that he might better cure it in himself, by his writings and observations teach others how to prevent and avoid it.'[8] There are echoes of this 'anatomising' of animals with the 'anatomy' that Burton constructs as his study of melancholy, the idea of trying to find the cause, and the cure. It is speculated that Burton's adoption of a pseudonym allowed him to present his own melancholy, that he was part and parcel of what was considered 'so universal a malady' and an 'epidemical disease' – words that carry a curious resonance amid today's concern over the pervasiveness of depression.

Samuel Johnson's definition of melancholy in his eighteenth-century *Dictionary* listed 'madness' amongst its senses. For Johnson, melancholy had no positive dimensions, no aspect of genius, and was a sign of insanity. In addition to his *Dictionary*, Johnson also compiled an extensive set of *Sermons*, where he provided a more thorough account of the madness of melancholy, particularly its effects. He believed melancholy to be the cause of fixating on one 'notion or inclination' so that it 'takes such an entire possession of a man's mind, and so engrosses his faculties, as to mingle thoughts perhaps he is not himself conscious of with almost all his conceptions, and influence his whole behavior.'[9]

While Samuel Johnson listed 'madness' amongst the definitions of *melancholy*, the nineteenth-century encyclopaedia of Good, Gregory and Bosworth, *Pantologia*, split the definition into two terms, adding a separate entry for *melancholia*. They retained Johnson's definition of melancholy in the senses of a literary, Shakespearean 'madness' or 'temper', but the 'disease' component was ascribed to *melancholia*. This, they defined as:

Melancholy madness. A disease in the class neuroses ... characterized by erroneous judgment ... from imaginary perceptions or recollections influencing the conduct, and depressing the mind with ill-grounded fears; not combined with either pyrexia [fever] or comatose affections; often appearing without dyspepsia, yet attended with costiveness [constipation], chiefly in persons of rigid fibres and torpid insensibility.[10]

Sigmund Freud established a further landmark in the map of melancholy and madness in 1917, with his essay *Mourning and Melancholia*. The difference between 'normal' and 'abnormal' grief is again the foundation for the distinctions he makes, with melancholia identified as a pathological condition, the state where mourning fails to reach completion. The individual, or ego, embeds their sense of loss within themselves, refusing to allow the loss to pass. Freud described how the '[t]he shadow of the object fell upon the ego' and 'the loss of the object had been transformed into the loss of ego', so that the loss of the object, whether it be a person or an idea, becomes the same as the loss of the self, the ego.[11] The melancholic remains attached to this loss, and does not seek a cure.

The rise of psychiatry and psychoanalysis had a major influence on the codification of melancholia, yet the definitions and distinctions remain stubbornly imprecise. In an effort to achieve clinical precision the signs of melancholy were transliterated into medical-speak, so that lethargy and listlessness, for example, became 'psychomotor retardation'.[12] Depression and bi-polarity became implicated within the discourse on melancholy, and the desire to objectify, and consequently 'treat', these conditions is symptomatic of the overall medicalisation of mental wellbeing. Yet, despite its inclusion in the authoritative DSM – the *Diagnostic and Statistical Manual of Mental Disorders* published by the American Psychiatric Association, the psychiatrist's 'bible' – debate still continues within psychiatry over the definition of melancholia.

The definition, and thus the diagnosis, of melancholia in the DSM is problematic, not least because it seeks to objectify something which is strongly coloured by subjectivity. The dilemma is the same as that embedded in the very origins of definitions of melancholia: who is to judge when sadness is disproportionate? Added to this are the flaws in definition that led to such situations as American and British psychiatrists using identical versions of the DSM, with exactly the same group of patients, making completely different diagnoses.

Psychiatry persists in attempts to codify melancholia, and recent debate includes such assertions as: 'melancholia, rather than being a dimensionally severe condition, is quintessentially a categorical condition awaiting prototypic definition as a category',[13] and this is necessary to avoid 'overdiagnosis' of melancholia. In other words, the ongoing lack of a clear definition allows for imprecision within the realm of the science of psychiatry, which like any science aspires to precision. As part of this debate, psychiatrists Fink and Taylor attempted a definition of melancholia via a list – an approach reminiscent of Robert Burton's *Anatomy of Melancholy* – which relied largely on definition through enumeration. In the category of 'melancholia' they listed 'Psychotic depression, Manic-depression, Puerperal depression, Abnormal bereavement, Depression with stupor or catatonia', and in 'Non-melancholic mood disorders' they placed 'Characterological depression, Reactive depressive disorders, Premenstrual dysphoria.'[14] It seems that science is far from reducing melancholia to a set of quantifiable, objective features, and its elusive quality sees it slipping out of any container into which it is placed.

However, psychiatric concerns cast the *Field Guide's* advocacy of melancholy as a rich dimension of human existence into tricky territory, with global worries over the increase in mental illness – of an escalation of melancholy seen as madness. Writers such as Peter D Kramer are emphatic that depression as a medical illness should be eradicated, just as diseases like smallpox have been. Kramer, a clinical professor of psychiatry at Brown University and author of *Listening to Prozac* and *Against Depression*, believes that there is a need to re-evaluate the whole tradition of 'heroic melancholy' which he sees as standing in the way of true depression, through providing excuses or validations for this condition. Yet, while Kramer writes melancholy off as a type of 'myth' it is also important to remain critical of science, which operates within its own mythology and 'truths'.

On the other hand, in *The Loss of Sadness,* a critique of the massive increase in depression, Allan V Horwitz and Jerome C Wakefield claim that it is a redefinition of depression rather than any shift in the populace's mental health, which explains the contemporary situation. Put simply, it is 'diagnostic inflation' based on a flawed definition.[15] Which is to say, 'the recent explosion of putative depressive disorder, in fact, does not stem primarily from a real rise in this condition. Instead it is a product of conflating the two conceptually distinct categories of normal sadness and depressive disorder and thus *classifying the many instances of normal sadness as mental disorders.'*[16]

Horwitz and Wakefield criticise the DSM for failing to align diagnoses of mental illness with 'context,' and thus 'normal' responses to stressors – things which might trigger mental illness – were being diagnosed as illness. While this might assist the psychiatrists in their categorisation, it threatens the central conundrum of melancholy: one of the key elements of its constellation is sadness-*without*-cause. Or in psychiatric-speak, depression-without-stressor.

Both Kramer's and Horwitz and Wakefield's work serve to further complicate the legacy of melancholy and madness. Psychiatry's efforts to draw a line between normal and abnormal sadness, and a wish to eradicate the latter, bring the worrying scenario that the baby will be thrown out with the bathwater. Melancholia has always been the paradox of 'the normally abnormal' and to normalise everything to some euphoric equilibrium threatens to eliminate the shadows within the human condition.

And, melancholia isn't universally homogenous. Although there is agreement that sadness is generic, melancholy is culturally inflected, and has been since its origins. The legacy of melancholia appears in both Western and Eastern writings, and while there are substantial agreements and complementarities, it is hardly a universal ill – like smallpox. There are arguments that 'melancholia' as 'clinical depression' is a construction of the West. Shushrut Jadhav asks, 'Is the indigenous Indian version of depression the same as western depression?' and provides the response: 'we do not know'.[17] The context differs across cultures, and melancholy might therefore vary in ways as subtle as an accent, or as profound as an entirely different lexicon, as explored in Chapter 4. And there is a politics of melancholia – a belief that each culture should have ownership of their interpretations and beliefs, as opposed to a globalised ethnopsychiatry.

A Field Guide to Melancholy does not romanticise depression, and is rather part of a salvage operation, reclaiming melancholy's bitter-sweetness. The reality and painfulness of major depression is undeniable, and many readers will be familiar with the plight of sufferers of depression and the need for treatment. The conflation of melancholy and depression, and the undefinitive definitions of melancholy as madness, reveal that there are still many shades of grey. While science pushes towards wanting to find clear-cut conditions, striving to determine that melancholy is binary rather than analogue (either you are or you aren't melancholy) the complexity of melancholy's mélange resists such cleaving. There are associated questions of morals and ethics which further complicate things, including whether treatments should be pharmaceutical or psychoanalytical, whether psychiatry is universally applicable, and so on, and this book will not seek to extend these particular arguments. Whether due to diagnostic inflation or a demonstrable psychopathological change in the population, the concern is that the creative capacity of melancholy will be suppressed because of the fear of madness, and along with the elimination of 'bad melancholy' comes the loss of the 'good melancholy' of genius and beauty.

Melancholy and Genius: 'A disease of heroes'

The connection between melancholy and the intellect is a circular one. Throughout melancholy's history the conundrum has been detected at various points on this circle – in some cases melancholy is seen as a cause of genius, and in others as a consequence of it. Irrespective of which is the cause and which the effect, the introspection of melancholy in the context of 'genius' is associated with unusual insight, in sharp distinction from that particular thread of the discourse which connects melancholy self-absorption with sloth, or *acedia*. The very same things which might be considered signs of madness, then, can also be interpreted as genius.

This paradox of melancholy and genius was first captured in Aristotle's 'Problem XXX, I',[18] which begins with the perplexing question, 'Why is it that all those who have become eminent in philosophy or politics or poetry or the arts are clearly melancholics, and some of them to the extent as to be affected by diseases caused by black bile?'[19] The 'problem' is outlined in a lengthy discussion on the varying manifestations of melancholy, including the 'air' produced by flatulence and sexual arousal, and concludes that 'all melancholy persons are out of the ordinary, not owing to illness, but from their natural constitution' – or as Klibansky, Panofsky and Saxl put it: 'normally abnormal'.[20]

The necessary balance needed to ensure a melancholic is not a freak but a genius is speculated to come from the correct amount of melancholy humour – black bile – and that it must be of an average temperature, not too hot, nor too cold. The melancholic genius navigates a path between the two great abysses of depression and recklessness. If the black bile is too cold the resulting melancholia is one of dullness, and too hot brings about melancholic mania – in between is the melancholic mean, the condition of genius.

Aulus Gellius's *Attic Nights*, from the middle of the second century AD, is one of the early, classic texts to document the association of melancholy and genius, or in Gellius's case, heroism. The 1795 edition of *Attic Nights* describes how 'the waywardness of disposition which is called melancholy' is something which does 'not happen to little and weak minds; but there is something of elevated affection in it.'[21] It also aligns melancholy with the idea of 'frenzy' and still further with the 'highest spiritual exaltation'.

Throughout history, oscillations have continued between madness, melancholy and intellect, with waves of interest such as the medieval scholar Albertus Magnus's work on Aristotle's 'Problem XXX, I' which re-awakened interest in the connections, re-stating the melancholic's outstanding qualities as good memory and astuteness. The two poles of this conundrum are positioned around the heavy gravitas of the saturnine temperament, and the contrasting *'spiritus phantasticus'* – the imaginative soul, the elusive creative spark of genius itself. Aristotle's conundrum sheds light upon the internal conflictions of an attraction to that which is sorrowful, and a co-dependence of positive and negative within melancholy. The recognition of an artistic temperament particularly associated with melancholy is the legacy of the Problem and, throughout history, there are examples of artists and writers whose best work was produced when they were afflicted with melancholy.

The idea of melancholy genius, or 'genial melancholy', was revived during the Renaissance. Melancholy had become less significant during the Middle Ages but, with the self-conscious perspective of humanism, melancholy became a significant attribute for Renaissance men. Once more reviving the ideas of Aristotle's problem, and of the

Neoplatonic sense of Saturn's auspicious nature, the intellectual elite came to see their melancholy as a 'privilege'. Philosopher Marsilio Ficino was a key influence on the development of ideas on genius and melancholy. In his *De vita libri tres,* or 'Three Books on Life', he brought together the opposing traditions of *furor melancholicus* and *furor divinus,* joining Aristotelian melancholy with Plato's concept of mania, the sacred fury or madness of creativity and inspiration.

The association of genius and melancholy is seen in the accounts of depressive artists, the 'mad artists', where melancholy is both the cause and effect of extreme creativity. Giorgio Vasari's documentation of the lives of artists in the sixteenth century captures the melancholy which fuelled the creative spark, or resulted from it. Paolo Uccello's focus on perfecting perspective choked his mind with difficult problems, explained Vasari, and filled him with the anxiety of pursuing minutiae, and like other such artists he ended up 'solitary, eccentric, melancholy and poor'.[22] Uccello's obsession with perspective exhibited the typical melancholy fixation on specific ideas. And Antonio da Correggio 'was very melancholy in the practice of his art, at which he toiled unceasingly.'[23] Raphael was 'inclined to melancholy like all men of such talent'[24], and in his majestic image of the *School of Athens,* 1509, he painted another melancholic, Michelangelo, whom he portrays as the pessimistic, 'weeping' philosopher Heraclitus, in the traditional melancholy pose with the head resting on the hand.

Dürer's image of *Melencolia I,* 1514, is perhaps the most iconic image of melancholy genius, expressing the ambivalence of scholasticism in opposition to sloth. On one

hand the figure of the angel appears sunk in contemplative thought, yet around her lie the tools of knowledge, as
though abandoned. These twin forces of melancholy are
the 'typus Acediae' and the 'typus Geometriae'. 'Acediae'
is slothfulness, and 'Geometriae' is not simply geometry as
such, but the broader idea of the scholasticism of the lib-
eral arts, of knowledge and learning. In Dürer's image,
however, the idleness is not sloth-like, but contemplative and preoccupied, reflecting his own melancholic
traits. The angel is a symbol of a melancholic 'winged
genius' who embodies melancholy's associations with
humanitarian concerns, noble solitude, and the contemplation of nature, the locus of a *tristitia utilis,* or 'useful sorrow', as advocated by Hugh of StVictor in his *Medicine of
the Soul.*[25]

With the re-recognition of its connection to genius in
Renaissance times, melancholy became something to be
aspired to and, with this social cachet, it became a type of
affectation. Michel de Montaigne, the sixteenth-century
essayist, observed the way in which melancholy was seen
as fodder, trivial. There were those who 'fed on melancholy', giving it the 'shadow of *friandise*' – like little sweet-
meats.[26]

Ben Jonson parodied this aspiration towards melancholy in his play *Every Man in his Humour*, 1598, part of
the tradition of 'comedies of humour' which explore the
humoral traits. Desiring the association between melancholy and genius, Mr Stephen asks for a stool to be
melancholy upon, and introduces himself as being 'might-
ily given to melancholy' in order to make an impression.
A response comes from an amateur poet, Mathew, who
also claims the genius of melancholy, 'Your true melan-

choly breeds your perfect fine wit, sir. I am melancholy myself, divers times, sir, and then do I no more but take pen and paper, presently, and overflow you half a score, or a dozen of sonnets at a sitting.' Still insecure in being sufficiently melancholy, Mr Stephen later checks with his more esteemed cousin Edward, '…is it well? Am I melancholy enough?'[27]

There is something of a hiatus between the melancholy artist geniuses (and wannabe geniuses) of the Renaissance and the later Romantic era painters and writers. In their extensive survey, *Born Under Saturn*, the Wittkowers note that the idea of the melancholic artist goes out of fashion between the seventeenth century and sometime around the work of Caspar David Friedrich, in the early nineteenth century. In between these times artists like Bernini, Rubens, Rembrandt and Velázquez were never described as melancholic and showed no trace of the affliction.[28]

The association with exceptional intellectual ability was again a significant thread of Romanticism, and the flowering of poetry during this time was steeped in melancholy. The Romantic poets and painters were characterised by moods and demeanours that were described as melancholy or depressive, conditions which were considered generators of artistic impulse. The key poets of Romanticism – William Blake, Samuel Taylor Coleridge, Lord Byron, Percy Bysshe Shelley and John Keats – are all believed to have suffered from depression. Byron's lines from *The Dream* capture the conundrum of melancholy as both madness and genius:

And this the world calls frenzy; but the wise
Have a far deeper madness, and the glance

Of melancholy is a fearful gift;
What is it but the telescope of truth?

'I wake and feel the fell of dark, not day', is the beginning of one of the darkest expressions of nineteenth-century genial melancholy, the words from Gerard Manley Hopkins' so-called 'terrible sonnets'. Hopkins' sonnets are a kind of depression memoir, an anguish born of religious melancholy. The terrible sonnets are an echo of the 'Dark Night of the Soul' of the sixteenth-century mystic, St John of the Cross, whose writings come from a period of confinement to a cell and are suffused with images of depression, sorrow and divine abandonment.

Other nineteenth-century and early twentieth-century geniuses are also linked with melancholy, notably the philosophers of modernity, Søren Kierkegaard and Walter Benjamin. Kierkegaard's mental state was described as 'depression, alternating with, but more commonly blended with, a condition of exaltation.'[29] He saw how pervasive this malady was and, in a sweepingly panoramic statement, presented the diagnosis that 'melancholia is the ailment of our age'.[30] The young Walter Benjamin was characterised by 'a profound sadness' according to Gershom Scholem, and he grew into a self-declared melancholic. Despite the impact of Freud's conceptualisation of melancholia at this time, Benjamin eschewed these fresh psychological ideas, and instead reclaimed the astrological legacy, declaring: 'I came into the world under the sign of Saturn – the star of the slowest revolution, the planet of detours and delays...'[31] Benjamin was a major theorist of melancholy, notably in his 1928 work on German *Trauerspiel* (tragedy or literally 'mourning play'), and his vast but never completed *Passagenwerk*, known in English as *The Arcades Project*. There was a seamlessness between his own internal condition and the topics that he applied himself to, excavating 'the Saturnine acedia' from the baroque theatre, revealing the presence of melancholy in literature as in Proust's 'loneliness which pulls the world down into its vortex', and identifying other melancholy geniuses like Franz Kafka who was 'essentially solitary'.[32]

Melancholic depression persisted throughout the two centuries as a common thread amongst creative geniuses – painters including Vincent Van Gogh, Henri de Toulouse-Lautrec, Jackson Pollock and Mark Rothko; writers Ernest Hemingway, Samuel Beckett, Edgar Allan Poe and Virginia Woolf; poets Charles Baudelaire, Rainer Maria Rilke and Emily Dickinson; and composers Ludwig van Beethoven, Frederic Chopin and Irving Berlin. The resonances between the artists' mind-states and their work is often quite transparent, such that the melancholy becomes writ large. In Emily Dickinson's poetry, for example, her 'winter within', the manifestation of the 'fixed melancholy' which had developed during adolescence, is seen as the major generative force in her poetry which is suffused with a poignant and brooding emotional climate.[33]

Consistent with melancholy's extraordinarily enduring constellation, the paradoxical relationship between melancholy and heroism or genius remains remarkably stable. Despite small apparent hiatuses, as in the time of Rembrandt and Velázquez mentioned above, the idea of melancholic genius provides a persistent thread in cultural history. Even the artistic and scientific poles of melancholy concur on the coincidence of exceptional creativity and the melancholic condition – irrespective of whether it is considered a mood or a mental illness allied with bipolar disorder. Two and a half thousand years after it was first documented, two psychiatrists set out to find proof of the original Aristotelian statement on genius and melancholy, the 'Problem XXX, I'. They concluded, 'the question of melancholia and intellectual and/or artistic eminence which has so preoccupied Western thought and art history... may hinge on mixity, the co-existence of hypomanic elements in melancholia... which itself derives from the intrusion into or intersection of cyclothymia and hyperthymia with melancholia.' The psychiatrists Akiskal and Akiskal explain that this is technically the realm of the 'bipolar spectrum' and they add that, 'In other words, manic-depressive illness, rather than subserving what is exceptional in human beings, appears to serve as the genetic reservoir of greatness. The price of greatness... is costly, but seems to reside in the subpsychotic interface of bipolar temperaments and affective disease, as hypothesized in the passage attributed to Aristotle.'[34]

Melancholy and Beauty: 'Spirited sadness'

The final conundrum of melancholy is an aesthetic one – why should the appearance of sadness hold aesthetic appeal? Morally, ethically, logically, it might be expected that sadness would not be associated with beauty. Yet, it is this very contradiction that contributes to melancholy's elevation above its early companions in the humoral tradition – the choleric, the sanguine and the phlegmatic. Beyond the fears of madness, and alongside ideas of genius, the aesthetic appeal of melancholy is central to its paradoxical attraction.

While melancholy's history is lengthy, the recognition of its beauty is relatively recent. There were glimmers of a melancholy beauty in the Dark Ages. The sixth-century philosopher Boethius observed that, 'The beauty of things is fleet and swift, more fugitive than the passing of flowers…'[35] The recognition of the beauty of things about to disappear, of the intensification of beauty at the approach of death, is a melancholic species called *ubi sunt*, Latin for 'where are?' The beauty of the *ubi sunt* moment is a version of nostalgic yearning and backwards-looking wonder at the fragility of what comes to pass.

By the sixteenth century the beauty of melancholy is clearly recognised and an avalanche of imagery and writing begins. Umberto Eco's *History of Beauty* plots the expression of 'melancholy beauty' at this time, pointing towards the iconic image of Dürer's *Melencolia I* as the emblem of this shift. Eco defines the ingredients for the creation of this 'melancholic Beauty' as the double attribution of melancholy and genius. While the association was a foundational one for melancholy – thinking back to Aristotle's 'Problem XXX, I' which asked why men of genius are melancholy – Eco emphasises that at this later point in time the flow went in two directions. The 'commingling of *ars geometrica* and *homo melancholicus*' gained the new aspect of beauty as 'geometry acquires a soul and melancholy a full intellectual dimension'.[36]

Looking back to the imagery of this time, Romanian philosopher EM Cioran finds that melancholy beauty has a subdued gracefulness that is not there in tragic and intense sadness. He writes of the 'strange sickly beauty' of melancholy and its 'passivity, dreaminess, and voluptuous enchantment'. Cioran finds it in the 'wide perspective of Dutch or Renaissance landscape, with its eternity of lights and shadows, its undulating vales symbolizing infinity, its transfiguring rays of light which spiritualize the material world and the hopes and regrets of men who smile wisely – the whole perspective breathes an easy melancholy grace.'[37] The important distinction for Cioran is between melancholy and sadness, in that pure sadness is irrevocable, while melancholy offers a future, a 'graceful dream'.

While melancholy was well established in the lyrical and pictorial traditions of the late sixteenth century, its significance later paled in the face of the eighteenth century's codification of the Sublime, the Beautiful and the Picturesque. Vigorous debate was focused on defining and categorising the nature of aesthetic experience and general ideas like 'beauty' gave way to more particular definitions. But melancholy was never elevated to a capitalised aesthetic type, nor given the definite article, like the other categories – there was never 'the Melancholy'. In the late eighteenth century Immanuel Kant designated the first two significant aesthetic domains, the Sublime and the Beautiful, both of which are, in themselves, immensely complex conditions.[38] The Sublime is that which is unbounded, beyond comprehension and awe-inspiring, and imparts feelings of horror. The Beautiful, on the other hand, brings feelings of joy and pleasure.

Kant relates the idea of sensation back to the humoral tradition, aligning aesthetic appreciation – or lack of it – with each of the four temperaments. The phlegmatic is considered to have a deficiency of finer sensation and a comparative apathy, and is dismissed as having no place in his study of aesthetics. The choleric, too, does not have a deep appreciation of aesthetics, tending to overemphasise the moral consequences of a fine feeling, but only at the level of the gloss. More in keeping with the idea of the beautiful is the character of the sanguine, who is not one-dimensional in his or her aesthetic appreciation, but is sensitive to the varied circumstances. The sanguine has adoptive virtues, which are the mark of nobility and compassion. Kant makes a distinction between these adoptive virtues, which are beautiful and charming, and the genuine virtues, described as sublime and venerable. It is with the genuine virtues that he associates melancholy. With a 'profound feeling for the beauty and human nature and a firmness and determination of the mind' the melancholy frame of mind is distinguished from the 'changeable gaiety' and inconstancy of a 'frivolous person'.[39] It is gentle and noble, and characterised by the sense of awe in apprehending a danger to be overcome and the aspiration towards self-conquest.

Melancholy is therefore associated with 'beauty' in its generalised sense, and also with Kant's particular category of the Sublime. This is further developed in *Critique of Judgment* (1790) in which he grappled with the predicament of solitude. He argued that on one hand the melancholy detachment of solitude can be considered Sublime if it is motivated by self-sufficiency and perhaps asceticism. But on the other hand, it is 'partly hateful and partly contemptible' if it is founded upon misanthropy. A Sublime sadness must be founded on ideas and could be found in a place of retreat, a place for contemplative solitude. As philosopher Dylan Trigg points out, this sense of the self in solitude is a primarily melancholy trait, 'The

awareness of the self and so necessarily the Other is…
accentuated in the melancholic: he is aware of all that he
isn't; and the sublime is always a contrast between micro-
scopic and macroscopic polarities – the greater this is
realised, the higher the sublimity.'[40]

Kant's place of solitude, the locus of melancholy, cannot be, however, 'so altogether inhospitable as only to af-
ford a most miserable retreat for a human being'.
Melancholy can take its place among the 'vigorous affections' only if it has a root in moral ideas, and not if it is a
dispirited sadness. And if it is grounded on sympathy, it
might be considered 'lovable', but only worthy of being
classed as a 'languid affection'.[41] A Kantian melancholy
might be therefore called a 'spirited sadness', one which
draws strength and conviction from a grounding within
moral ideas. So while Kant makes efforts to connect
melancholy to the Sublime, he also reveals the difficult
conundrum of finding aesthetic appeal in melancholy.

The aesthetic debates became further complicated by
the arrival of a third specific category: the Picturesque.
Ongoing definitions of this category were increasingly
focused on the landscape, in terms of both its design and
appreciation. Picturesque theory is a richly complex topic
but, in very general terms, it is based upon the idea of
finding a specific kind of beauty defined in pictures –
notably those by seventeenth-century artists Claude Lor-
rain, Salvator Rosa and Nicholas Poussin. These works
captured scenes of landscapes worked over by history, and
steeped in culture, thereby setting up a desire for elements
like ruins, signs of the sublimity of nature's wrath such as
dead trees, and a pastoral aesthetic of open park-like landscapes. This affected both how the landscape was shaped

in the making of gardens, and what was sought in the landscape, which initiated the idea of picturesque tourism – of going on holiday to look at 'scenery' – that persists today.

However, there was again a conflicted position similar to that encountered by Kant in his efforts to distinguish a morally defensible version of melancholy appreciation, from one which was either immoral or merely languid. An aesthetic category which favoured objects like ruins and dead trees became a problem, even more so once these same qualities were extended to other domains. While the late eighteenth-century theorists, including Richard Payne Knight and Uvedale Price, could defend the melancholy attraction of picturesque ruins, it became perverse when applied to people. Could those same signs of decay be found to be melancholically beautiful in a person? Price reflected that if such a woman was afflicted by the signs of irregularity that he could wax lyrical about in the landscape, 'You will hardly find a man fond enough of the picturesque to marry a girl so thoroughly de-formed.'[42]

The Picturesque came to operate more as an anaes-thetic than an aesthetic in such cases, suspending an eth-ical response in favour of a delight in what is beheld. Nineteenth-century art and architectural critic, John Ruskin, called this conundrum the 'heartless picturesque', in distinction from the 'noble picturesque' which he saw in the works of JMW Turner and Samuel Prout. Herman Melville termed this conflicted attraction to melancholy scenes 'povertiresque' in his 1852 novel *Pierre*. This is the soulless version of beauty which is the quarry of the 'hunters of the picturesque', those who see without feeling, where aesthetics numbs ethics. Ruskin's unease in finding aesthetic pleasure in scenes of poverty, of 'delight in ruins', is evident in his description of wandering amongst the slum-dwellers of Amiens, who seemed 'all exquisitely picturesque, and no less miserable... Seeing the unhealthy face and melancholy mien... I could not help feeling how many suffering persons must pay for my picturesque subject and happy walk.'[43]

The immoral, predatory, version of melancholy beauty, the aesthetic of 'miserable' sadness, is epitomised by Charles Dickens' character Will Fern in *The Chimes*. Will, 'a poor and honest man, but who has been given a bad name', emphasises the potential danger in the conundrum of finding beauty in melancholy suffering. His home is a leaky hovel, and evidently a popular subject for picturesque sketching, and he declares, 'You may see the cottage from the sunk fence over yonder. I've seen the ladies draw it in their books, a hundred times. It looks well in a picter, I've heerd say; but there ain't weather in picters, and maybe 'tis fitter for that, than for a place to live in. Well! I lived there. How hard – how bitter hard, I lived there, I won't say.'[44]

Will Fern is an early victim of what became known as the 'culture of spectatorship' – the fascination with scenes of suffering. Susan Sontag described how 'the appetite for pictures showing bodies in pain is as keen, almost, as the desire for ones that show bodies naked.'[45] The aestheticising of poverty and pain is an expression of *schadenfreude*, a narcosis that sees beholders suspend emotional responses in favour of finding aesthetic pleasure. Delighting in melancholy despair can be seen in the 'beauty' of Heroin Chic – the near-death, white-skin, black-eyes look of drug addiction that was popularised by model Kate Moss in the Calvin Klein advertising campaigns of the 1990s. Heroin Chic could be imagined in the landscape as well. The starkly melancholic beauty of someone who seems near death is analogous to the aesthetic fascination with landscapes which are devastated in some way. A dark beauty is found in scenes of landscapes of war, of the ravages of mining, and in toxic and ruined post-industrial landscapes. Chapter 5 returns to this theme, exploring the work of photographers including Bernd and Hiller Becher and Edward Burtynsky.

The aestheticising of melancholy objects, as in a model who appears nearly dead, a dilapidated cottage, or a ruined post-industrial landscape, involves a process of detachment. Through this, the object is set apart, as Susan Sontag described in *Melancholy Objects,* and it then becomes like a 'found object', and the focus of fascination. This is the species of melancholy beauty that was the foundation of surrealism. In its super-realism, or verisimilitude, surrealism evoked the strange in the terms of the familiar. The uncanny place of the dream-world hovered on the edge of reality, unlikely juxtapositions and hybrids emphasised the feelings of alienation and isolation of the modern human condition.

This potent, elusive beauty is a unique quality of melancholy, and one at the polar extreme to the aesthetic delight of that which brings joy. Edgar Allan Poe pronounced sadness and melancholy the sites of Beauty's 'highest manifestation', and as death is the supreme melancholy topic, then its poetical potency is enhanced when aligned with beauty. Poe's 'beauty' was no superficial superlative, but referred to an effect upon the self, 'that intense and pure elevation of the *soul* – *not* of intellect, or of the heart'.[46] Such a complete immersion in the connection of beauty and melancholy was echoed in the words of the poet Charles Baudelaire. He confines all beauty to that connected to sadness, and his words seal the conundrum of melancholy and beauty: 'I have found a definition of the Beautiful, of my own conception of the Beautiful. It is something intense and sad, something a little vague, leaving scope for conjecture.' Baudelaire relates this beauty directly to that found in a face, which in its voluptuousness is 'all the more attractive the more the face is melancholy'. And this beautiful head suggests ardours, passions, repressed ambitions, mystery and unhappiness. Baudelaire explains, 'I do not pretend Joy cannot associate with Beauty, but I will maintain that Joy is one of her most vulgar adornments while Melancholy may be called her illustrious spouse – so much so that I can scarcely conceive… a type of Beauty which has nothing to do with Sorrow.'[47]

Notes

1. Jim Jarmusch, *Down by Law*, film written by Jarmusch, cited in Mark Montandon, *Innocent When You Dream: The Tom Waits Reader*, frontispiece.
2. Oribasius of Pergamon (325-403 AD) in Stanley W Jackson, *Melancholia and Depression: From Hippocratic Times to Modern Times*, p.51.
3. ibid, p.54.
4. Jan Weir cited in Claudia Swan, *Art, Science and Witchcraft in Early Modern Holland*, p.159.
5. Mary Ann Jimenez, 'Madness in Early American History: Insanity in Massachusetts from 1700-1830', p.31.
6. ibid.
7. Robert Burton, *The Anatomy of Melancholy* – there are numerous

editions of the book, including digitised versions online from a range of editions.

8. Robert Burton, *An Anatomy of Melancholy*, p.6.

9. Samuel Johnson quoted in Thomas Kass, *Morbid Melancholy, the Imagination and Samuel Johnson's Sermons*, p.50.

10. John Mason Good, Olinthus Gregory and Newton Bosworth, *Pantologia: A New Cabinet Cyclopaedia, Comprehending a Complete Series of Essays, Treatises and Systems, Alphabetically Arranged, with a General Dictionary of Arts, Sciences, and Word*, Vol. 7, no page numbers.

11. Sigmund Freud, *On Murder, Mourning and Melancholia*, p.209.

12. Sushrut Jadhav, 'The Cultural Origins of Western Depression', p.276.

13. Gordon Parker, 'The DSM Classification of Depressive Disorders: Debating Its Utility', p.872.

14. M Fink and MA Taylor, 'Resurrecting melancholia', Table 2, p.16.

15. Allan V Horwitz and Jerome C Wakefield, *The Loss of Sadness: How Psychiatry transformed Normal Sorrow into Depressive Disorder*, p.7.

16. ibid p.6, my emphasis.

17. Sushrut Jadhav, 'The Cultural Origins of Western Depression', p.281.

18. Sometimes ascribed to Pseudo-Aristotle to indicate doubts over attribution.

19. In Klibansky, Panofsky and Saxl, p.18.

20. ibid p.30.

21. Aulus Gellius, *Attic Nights*, p.345.

22. Giorgio Vasari, *The Lives of the Artists*, p.95.

23. ibid, p.278.

24. Rudolf and Margot Wittkower, *Born Under Saturn: The Character and Conduct of Artists: A Documented History from Antiquity to the French Revolution*, p.104.

25. See Giorgio Agamben, *Stanzas*, p.13.

26. Michael Andrew Screech and Marc Fumaroli, *Montaigne and Melancholy: The Wisdom of the Essays*, p.25.

27. Ben Johnson, *Five Plays*, pp.42-43.

28. Rudolf and Margot Wittkower, *Born Under Saturn: The Character and Conduct of Artists: A Documented History from Antiquity to the French Revolution*, p.106.

29. Walter Lowrie, *Kierkegaard*, p.98.

30. Søren Kierkegaard quoted in Theodor Adorno, *Kierkegaard: Construction of the Aesthetic,* p.60.

31. Walter Benjamin quoted in Susan Sontag, *Under the Sign of Saturn*, p.111.

32. ibid.

33. See for example John F McDermott, *Emily Dickinson Revisited: A Study of Periodicity in Her Work.*

34. Hagop S Akiskal and Kareen K Akiskal, 'In search of Aristotle: Temperament, human nature, melancholia, creativity and eminence', p.4.

35. Boethius, *The Consolations of Philosophy*, cited in Umberto Eco, *Art and Beauty in the Middle Ages*, p.9.

36. Umberto Eco, *History of Beauty*, p.226.

37. EM Cioran, *On the Heights of Despair*, p.32.

38. See Immanuel Kant, *Observations on the Feeling of the Beautiful and Sublime.*

39. ibid pp.63–64.

40. Dylan Trigg, *Schopenhauer and the Sublime Pleasure of Tragedy*, p.168.

41. Immanuel Kant, *The Critique of Judgment* (trans. John T. Goldthwait), p.162. The other common translation, by JH Bernard, uses the word 'depression' in place of melancholy in this passage, and refers to such emotions as 'sturdy' rather than vigorous, see Immanuel Kant, *The Critique of Judgment*, p.117.

42. Uvedale Price cited in David Lowenthal, *The Past is a Foreign Country,* p.166.

43. John Ruskin, *Modern Painters*, cited in ibid. And see also, E T Cook and Alexander Wedderburn, *The Works of John Ruskin*, Volume VI, pp.16-23.

44. Charles Dickens, *The Chimes,* pp.131-132.

45. Susan Sontag, *Regarding the Pain of Others*, p.41.

46. Elisabeth Bronfen, *Over Her Dead Body: Death, Femininity and the Aesthetic*, p.61.

47. Charles Baudelaire, *Intimate Journal*, pp.11-12.

The Hunt for Melancholy

Laurence Aberhart, *Oamaru, Otago, 18 April 1999*

2

The Hunt for Melancholy

I know why I am sad, but I do not know why I am melancholy.
EM Cioran, *On the Heights of Despair*[1]

Melancholy's elusory nature makes it difficult to pin down. Yet, there are certain qualities, characteristics, sensations, that are recognisable as melancholy. The identifying features of melancholy evolve from traditions of physiognomy, mythological associations, literary constructions, and artistic conventions. Melancholy is not only found in individuals, but across the spectrum of environmental experience and expression, in particular places and at certain times.

The Face of Melancholy

From early times there were strongly formed ideas about the appearance of melancholy in individuals, especially in the development of the ideas on physiognomy, where appearance was believed to relate to a person's character. Melancholy was manifested in those who were thin, dark, and hirsute with prominent veins. In late medieval times, for example, the characteristic melancholic was personified in Maistre Alain Chartier's invention of 'Dame Mérencolye', with her way of speaking slowly, her drooping lip, and a sense of weightiness in her complexion.

The way in which melancholy is reflected in posture

and actions, immediately brings to mind a couple of iconic art works – Albrecht Dürer's *Melencolia I* (1514) and Vincent Van Gogh's *Portrait of Dr Gachet* (1890). Dürer's image is perhaps the most iconic melancholic work of all, in which a curiously androgynous angel sits amongst an array of geometrical tools and objects, alongside other enigmatic forms such as a giant polyhedron, a ladder, and a sphere – all of which have been the subject of many lengthy analyses. The angel is often referred to as a female, for example by Frances Yates[2], but two important observers, Jean-Luc Marion[3] and Jean Clair[4], emphatically refer to the angel as male. Van Gogh's painting is also a landmark melancholy work, and depicts his own doctor, who is a melancholic himself. In both cases the subjects sit in what is called the *gestus melancholicus,* the gesture or posture of head-in-hands, diagnosed in the case of Van Gogh's *Dr Gachet*, as 'the classical depressive pose'.[5]

The motif of head-in-hands has a lengthy ancestry, and is found as much in the mourners in Egyptian sarcophagi relief images, as in medieval expressions of sorrow. The gesture represents a triad of 'grief, fatigue and meditation',[6] the cornerstones of melancholic demeanour. In both Dürer's and Van Gogh's images, the fist is clenched, and held against the head. The clenching of a fist had earlier been considered the sign of particular mental afflictions but here, held close to the head itself, becomes expressive of the anguish of the melancholic, fraught with the paradoxes and tensions of madness, genius, beauty, and so on. As Van Gogh wrote of his portrait of Dr Gachet, he showed him, 'Sad but gentle, yet clear and intelligent.'[7]

The eyes in melancholy have a particular quality, 'motionless, and directed either towards the earth or to some distant point, and the look is askance, uneasy and suspicious'.[8] This gaze can denote an otherworldly connection, as in that of Dürer's *Melencolia*, in which her 'eyes stare into the realm of the invisible with the same vain intensity as that with which her hand grasps the impalpable.'[9] Even the eyebrows might be melancholy, as in what the Chinese call *Chou mei*, or 'worry brows'.

Shakespeare was an astute observer of melancholy and is believed to have studied Timothy Bright's protopsychiatric *Treatise of Melancholy* (1586) in forming the character of Hamlet. In his soliloquy Hamlet offers a small catalogue of melancholy traits, clothing and demeanour:

> 'Tis not alone my inky cloak, good mother,
> Nor customary suits of solemn black,
> Nor windy suspiration of forced breath,
> No, nor the fruitful river in the eye,
> Nor the dejected haviour of the visage,
> Together with all forms, moods and shapes of grief,
> That can denote me truly...[10]

In particular, Hamlet announces two specific colourings of melancholy, inky and solemn black, in a description which also evokes the more recent dark and melancholy figure of Batman. The 'dark' version of Batman – as opposed to the commercialised television incarnation – is suffused with a tragic sense, with his darkened face and black cape. His brooding introspection, contrasted with 'heroic' qualities, makes him the epitome of melancholy, a latter-day Prince of Denmark.

A range of colours is associated with the manifestation

of melancholy, from those in colloquial terms like 'the blues' and 'a brown study', to those in the traditions of the ancient visualisation of melancholy as blue in the evocation of the sea, and as white because of the association with funerary decoration. Green and yellow coloured the melancholic portraits of the Elizabethan era,[11] and Shakespeare wrote of 'green and yellow melancholy', which is thought to suggest jealousy tinged with hope.[12] EM Cioran believed that, 'Blue is a soothing color for melancholy; it is neutral towards divinity. When God's call breaks through the azure, we would rather have heavy black clouds.'[13] 'Red melancholy' is associated with the image 'The Melancholy' by Lucas Cranach the Elder (1533), with connotations of eros, desire, and jealousy. Akiskal and Akiskal define the red-clothed woman in Cranach's image as having a gaze which is 'rather naughty',[14] and Frances Yates relates the image to witchcraft.[15] 'White melancholy' by contrast is a more serene state, evocative of an elegiac sadness, and becoming overwhelmed by one's own sensibility. In a letter to his friend Richard West in 1742, the poet Thomas Gray described his white melancholy, 'Mine, you are to know, is a white melancholy... which though it seldom laughs or dances, nor ever amounts to what one calls joy or pleasure, yet is a good easy sort of state and *ça ne laisse que de s'amuser*. The only fault of it is insipidity, which is apt now and then to give a sort of *ennui*, which makes one form certain little wishes that signify nothing...'[16]

Black, however, dominates descriptions of the presence of melancholy, as evoked by the moniker of Winston Churchill's depression: the 'black dog.' Even the very appearance of the melancholic was brooding and black. As

Frances Yates explains, 'the melancholic was dark in complexion, with black hair and a black face [i.e. swarthy] – the facies nigra or livid hue induced by the black bile of the melancholy complexion.'[17]

Yates's description also suggests the contemporary figure of the melancholic – the Emo. With hair dyed black and falling over the face in a long fringe across one eye, Emos, an abbreviated form of 'emotional', embody a melancholy aesthetic. Like many subcultures, their fashions, hairstyles and music reflect their preoccupations and, for Emos, this is the fetishisation of depression, sadness, and detachment. The subculture of the Emo is reminiscent of the affectation of melancholy around the seventeenth and eighteenth centuries, where it was seen as a desirable state because of its association with genius, as with Ben Jonson's 'Mr Stephen' encountered in Chapter 1. And, like the cult of 'heroin chic' where followers aspired to a condition which suggests unwellness, the Emo seeks to display the signs of melancholia's darkness, sometimes to the extent of self-disfigurement through the cutting of skin.

The demeanour of the dreamer is also associated with the presence of melancholy. French philosopher Gaston Bachelard in *The Poetics of Reverie* traces the relationship of melancholy and day dreaming, or reverie. He does not consider the presence of melancholy as a depressive influence, but that in a reverie tinged with melancholy it is an 'engaging melancholy which gives a continuity to our repose'.[18] Bachelard's sense of melancholy infusing the state of dreaming is captured in his quoting of Victor Hugo, 'For a long time, I remained motionless, letting myself be penetrated gently by this unspeakable ensemble, by the serenity of the sky and the melancholy of the moment.'[19] The direction of the eyes and mind away from the world is the inner contemplative space of melancholy.

Various occupations align themselves with melancholy. In another of Shakespeare's characteristic litanies, from *As You Like It*, Act 4, Scene 1, the so-called 'Melancholy Jaques' – sometimes considered a trial version of the character of Hamlet – sets out a spectrum of melancholic types in defining his own melancholy:

I have neither the scholar's melancholy, which is emulation; nor the musician's, which is fantastical; nor the courtier's, which is proud; nor the soldier's, which is ambitious; nor the lawyer's, which is politic; nor the lady's, which is nice; nor the lover's, which is all these; but it is a melancholy of mine own, compounded of many simples, extracted from many objects, and, indeed, the sundry contemplation of my travels; in which my often rumination wraps me in a most humorous sadness.[20]

In addition to this roll call of melancholics should be added historians, specifically art historians,[21] astronomers, weavers, and clowns. Such activities all require a certain degree of introspection, a sense of the vastness and incomprehensibility of things, and of memory and history. A preoccupation with the task of making endless recordings is one of melancholy's conundrums, as Jean Clair observed, 'The measurement of space and time is an infinite project, inspiring those who undertake it with a feeling of powerlessness, which leads to melancholy.'[22] Anything involving collection invites the fear of finality, and the melancholic needs closure to be eternally delayed, as Jean Baudrillard puts it, '*The collection is never really initiated in order to be completed* ... Whereas the acquisition of the final item would in effect denote the death of the subject.'[23]

Susan Sontag's evocation of Sir William Hamilton in *The Volcano Lover* is one such melancholy collector, in his youth collecting coins, automata, and musical instruments, then moving onto his significant collection of paintings. Sir William believed that, 'Collecting expresses a free-floating desire that attaches and re-attaches itself – it is a succession of desires. The true collector is in the grip not of what is collected but of collecting.'[24] Artist Tacita Dean conveys this paradoxical relationship with the act of collecting, 'Now the problem with a collection is realising that you've started one. Recently I have begun, quite unintentionally, to collect old postcards thematically. It started with finding an attractive postcard of a frozen water fountain. On finding the second frozen water fountain, I had begun a collection... You've started so you must continue, and with most collections, there is no end. Whether it is postcards of lighthouses or four-leaf clovers, there can never be the definitive collection. For what is more inert than a finished collection.'[25] This evasion of closure is at the heart of melancholy, and if there were to be a mascot for melancholy, which might be particularly beloved of the collectors, it would be Sisyphus.[26]

The sense of a daunting infinitude and attention to overwhelming detail in such tasks as collecting generates a feeling of irresolvability that is conducive to melancholy. This is echoed in WG Sebald's description of the internal agonies that come from complicated tasks of concentration:

That weavers in particular, together with scholars and writers with whom they had much in common, tended to suffer from melancholy and all the evils associated with it, is understandable given the nature of their work, which forced them to sit bent over, day after day, straining to keep their eyes on the complex patterns they created. It is difficult to imagine the depths of despair into which those can be driven who, even after the end of the working day are engrossed in their intricate designs and who are pursued, into their dreams, by the feeling that they have got hold of the wrong thread.[27]

Clowns, too, are potent exemplars of melancholy's contradictory nature. The happy face of the clown, the court jester, or the mime artist, is a means of overlaying a type of detachment, sadness even, with a self-mocking mask. As Klibansky, Panofsky and Saxl explained, 'the most perfect synthesis of profound thought and poetic wistfulness is achieved when true humour is deepened by melancholy; or, to express it the opposite way, when true melancholy is transfigured by humour.'[28] In *Vertigo*, WG Sebald's character Lukas is described as someone who 'was ever more frequently assailed by dark moods' but had been the official village clown, holding the office of carnival jester uncontested.[29]

Usually without speaking, clowns evoke pathos through their often seemingly unwitting humour, as in Italo Calvino's definition of melancholy as 'sadness that has taken on lightness', and melancholy and humour as 'inextricably intermingled'.[30] Antoine Watteau's imagery of the French clown archetype, Pierrot, illustrates the double-sided character. Known also as the 'Gilles,' Pierrot, in the eighteenth-century paintings by Watteau, became the symbolic melancholic clown. In pantomimes and at fêtes, Pierrot, often with white face and red mouth, represented a caricature of a 'happy' face, veiling a sad visage. Watteau's iconic image, known as 'Pierrot-Watteau', inspired the Romantic group of Théophile Gautier, Gérard de Nerval and Charles Baudelaire. Through their writings and imaginings the Pierrot-Watteau emblem morphed, gradually changing to the more tragic figure of Pierrot-Lunaire – the Pierrot of the moonlight. The mask began to give way to reveal a skull beneath, the presence of death. The Pierrot figure endures as the epitome of the melancholy clown, reappearing for example in Picasso's series of Harlequins, unmasked, and suffused with sorrow.

Marcel Marceau's miming, was a further echo of the poignant Pierrot. Again characterised by white face makeup, and the sense of a suppressed tragic dimension, Marceau also evoked the sadness embedded within a particular approach to humour. In an interview he once said, 'I try to be deep in my art form, to bring laughters [sic], melancholy.'[31] Marceau had a connection with Charlie Chaplin, sharing the manner of exaggerated actions and stylised gestures that conveyed ideas without words, particularly in the character Bip the Clown. And when the two met, in 1967, Marceau saw in Chaplin 'a sort of *tristesse*, a melancholy' which epitomises the undercurrent of sadness within the role of the clown, in miming, and in slapstick.

As the figure marooned on the outside of society, clowns become symbolic of latent tragedy – of imminent disaster. Søren Kierkegaard's tale of the clown in the theatre captures this melancholic predicament, of how being the eternal funny guy draws a veil over anything possibly serious. When a fire broke out backstage in the theatre, Kierkegaard recounts, 'the clown came out to warn the public, they thought it was a joke and applauded. He repeated it; the acclaim was even greater.'[32]

More recently, the melancholy clown is resurrected in Swiss artist Ugo Rondinone's conceptual art. Like Pierrot, Rondinone uses the mask of the clown as both an antidote and a platform for melancholy. In his performance-based art, Rondinone usually deploys actors to take on the clown role. Assuming positions of lassitude, they make a marked contrast to the energetic hilarity of the clichéd circus clown, and through this they point up the melancholy dimensions of the clown: 'loneliness, isolation, abandonment, persisting passivity and lethargy.'[33] In her discussion of Rondinone's clown works, Christine Ross explains how the tragic destiny derives from the condition of 'not being seen' – of the separation and disengagement between the clown and the viewers.

The clowns' attempts at *not being seen,* as an affected oblivion, are reminiscent of strategies of camouflage, of disappearing into the background. But as is typical of melancholy, a paradox always ensues: the clown, at the same time as camouflaging himself, becomes an exhibitionist. He wants to display his hidden qualities, he wants *to be seen not being seen.* This resonates with the way that early twentieth-century French sociologist Roger Caillois connected psychasthenia – a psychological disorder characterised by phobias and obsession – with the theory of camouflage. The famous essay by Callois, 'Mimicry and

Legendary Psychasthenia', brings clowning to mind, in the work of the mimic. By trying not to be seen, while still wanting to be seen, clowns set up an irony, where it is their camouflage that makes them vulnerable, like the insects in Caillois' essay, where:

> there are cases in which mimicry causes the creature to go from bad to worse: geometer-moth caterpillars simulate shoots of shrubbery so well that gardeners cut them with their pruning shears. The case of the Phyllia is even sadder: they browse among themselves, taking each other for real leaves…[34]

So, the face of melancholy, of the clowns, the weavers, and the scholars, is one which at once conceals and reveals the place of the individual in their world. Often contemplative, with furrowed brow and darkened face, the melancholic demeanour is detached, introspective. The typical melancholic tasks might involve activities of great detail and even greater infinitude, and a contradictory relationship with one's surroundings, like the melancholy of camouflaged insects themselves, who graze upon one another as a consequence of their own disguise. But, if these are the characteristics of individuals, where might we seek out melancholy?

The Place of Melancholy

The attributes of melancholy are not confined to the characteristics of a person, but can also be recognised in cities and landscapes. This shift from only being associated with people into broader categories grew out of late medieval times, and became particularly pronounced from the seventeenth century onwards, as 'sensibility' developed, emotional colourings were recognised in places, and even the quality of light might evoke a 'mood'. This was really a critical moment for melancholy, emphasising it as an exceptional concept, one which had superseded its former companions in phlegmatic, sanguine and choleric dispositions. Through being transferred beyond the individual into the things of the world it became an expansive idea, far beyond a mere pathological condition.

Places might be melancholy through association, where a site's history of tragic events can elicit feelings of sorrow. Or the melancholy may be induced by the more intangible qualities of a place, in the quality of light, the presence of water, plaintive birdsong.   John Evelyn, English writer and gardener, on visiting the Park at Bruxelles in the mid-seventeenth century identified the aspects of its melancholy nature: 'so naturally is it furnish'd with whatever may make it agreeable, melancholy and country-like. Here is a stately herony, divers springs of water, artificial cascades, rocks and grotts.'[35] Evelyn also found Groombridge 'a pretty melancholy seat, well wooded and water'd',[36] and Mr Sheldon's garden near Weybridge was also pretty in its melancholy.[37] For the poet and philosopher Alexander Pope, it was the 'hanging hills, whose tops were edged with groves, and whose feet water'd with winding rivers' in the Chilterns that had the 'most of that melancholy which once used to please [him]'.[38]

Melancholy traits can be transferred between the idea of the individual's qualities and those of the city through analogy, as in Orhan Pamuk's *Istanbul*. As in Freud's association of the palimpsest-like city of Rome with the cumulative nature of memory, Pamuk draws sharp comparisons between the city of Istanbul and the quintessentially Turkish character. Most significantly he finds this in its quality of *hüzün* – the Turkish melancholy. The *Field Guide* returns to *hüzün,* as part of the exploration of various cultural inflections of melancholy in Chapter 4, and to Pamuk's book itself in Chapter 5, but at this point it is important to plot Istanbul as one of melancholy's haunts. Pamuk makes the point that the *hüzün* of Istanbul is a similar yet different quality to that described by Robert Burton, for example, in his seventeeth-century *Anatomy of Melancholy*. Burton's melancholy, Pamuk explains, is a quality inherent in individuals, but *hüzün* is collective, and embedded in the place. So he finds the city as one great entity experiencing this melancholy, and that it is something that 'by paying our respects to [*hüzün's*] manifestations in the city's streets and views and people that we at last come to sense it everywhere: on cold winter mornings, when the sun suddenly falls on the Bosphorus and that faint vapour begins to rise from the surface, the *hüzün* is so dense that you can almost touch it, almost see it spread like a film over its people and landscapes.'[39]

London, too, is a haunt of melancholy, of layered histories, cultural impressions, and the quality of light, all of which contribute to a sense of poignancy, and even perhaps bleakness. Melancholy suffuses the monochromatic monologue of Patrick Keiller's film *London*, where the nameless narrator reflects upon the city's sense of pathos in the early 1990s. At a time of IRA bombings and a pervasive presence of socio-economic failings, Keiller's *London* is evoked almost as a ruin. Indeed a mark of the film is the pronouncement of certain parts of the city as 'monuments', as though its time has already passed.

London as a city of historic sediment conducive to melancholy is also evoked in books like Iain Sinclair's *Lights out for the Territory,* where 'a melancholy futurist poetic begins to operate: visionary street scenes unrivalled since the birth of cinema… the City is at last able to compose its own poetry, with no human intervention.'[40] Or in Peter Ackroyd's trans-temporal *Hawksmoor,* with its 'shaddowes' and brooding sensibility, one where the architecture itself is suffused with a melancholy demeanour, as well as the eighteenth-century characters' 'melancholick' troubles and 'melancholly vapours', counterpointed with the melancholy felt by the late twentieth-century detective, wandering in East London's winter light.[41] The parallel time periods that Ackroyd enlists in tale telling express the idea of time persisting in the layered sediments of London, an idea anticipated decades earlier in WB Yeats' lament, of his grievances about 'this melancholy London – I sometimes imagine that the souls of the lost are compelled to walk through its streets perpetually. One feels them passing like a whiff of air.'[42]

Countries too, as well as cities, lend themselves variously to the hunt for melancholy. England as a whole is identified with melancholy, both in its landscape and its people – 'The *English* are naturally Fanciful, and very often disposed by that Gloominess and Melancholy of temper, which is so frequent in our Nation, to many wild Notions and Visions to which others are not so liable ….', declared Joseph Addison in his 'Pleasures of the Imagination' piece in the *Spectator,* 1712.[43] Centuries later, novelist Natalia Ginzburg stated, 'England is beautiful and melancholy. I don't know many countries but I begin to suspect that England is the most melancholy country in the world.'[44]   In her perspective as an Italian, Ginzburg finds perhaps a different 'gloominess' to Addison, but in her 'Eulogy and Lament' she provides an inventory of England's melancholy gloom: it is there in the railway stations, which are the 'most openly gloomy', in the 'extremely gloomy' suburbs with their streets of little houses, and in the precise approach to planning everything down to the position of the last tree that makes its 'beauty seem sad'.

New Zealand also exhibits a particularly melancholy character. Actor Sam Neill once conducted a cinematic national psychoanalysis in his documentary about New Zealand films, which he called *Cinema of Unease*.[45] Highlighting the prevailing dark themes of violence, desolation and abandonment, Neill conveyed a melancholy underside to a nation often viewed from outside as a clean and green paradise. The brooding, rain-swept landscape of the West Coast in Mike Newell's film *Bad Blood* (1981), and the achingly introspective Taranaki setting of Vincent Ward's *Vigil* (1984), characterise a landscape and people of a dark melancholy. Or in Neill's own words about Jane Campion's film, *The Piano* and its expression of people and place: 'romantic, gothic, unique'. The literature of New Zealand also emphasises the experiences of isolation and abandonment, from John Mulgan's *Man Alone,* of which even the title encapsulates melancholy disengagement, to the psychological traumas in the novels of Janet Frame. And just as Sam Neill found in the long and lonely roads a certain sense of an 'indifferent landscape', an 'isolated space', the empty landscapes extend right into the towns themselves. The rudimentary small townships are still havens for memory, yet their almost fugitive character lends a feeling of vulnerability, fragility, to them. Author Martin Edmond divines the 'small town melancholy' in the work of an earlier New Zealand writer, Ronald Hugh Morrieson. In Morrieson's first book *The Scarecrow*, there are spaces that evoke the sense of things gone awry, of dead dreams, of places 'inhabited by sorrow and loss'.[46]

Melancholy's multifarious nature allows it to haunt a range of locales. While the *Field Guide* can't provide an exhaustive list of settings, England and New Zealand represent two distinct typologies. England's melancholy was traditionally a romantic one, from the age of Picturesque gardens and journeys, and the lyrical literary moments, later overlaid with the *ennui* of modernity. In New Zealand the melancholy has tended toward a gothic, brooding quality, where the pioneering spirit encountered the *genius loci*, the spirit of the place. Emotion flowed from the country's spectacular natural scenery, bringing forth the awe of the Sublime and the solitude of melancholy. There are echoes of these various melancholic colourings around the world, and these examples are a means of pointing at some things to allow others to be recognised. For example, extending this thread of melancholy encounters with natural scenery brings us quickly to Australia, where Marcus Clarke in his *Australia Tales* asked, 'What is the dominant note of Australian Scenery? That which is the dominant note of Edgar Allan Poe's poetry – Weird Melancholy.'[47] He said a poem like *L'Allegro* could never be written there, singling out Milton's 'happy' half of the pair of poems, of which the melancholy half is *Il Penseroso*. Clarke catalogued Australian mountain forests as: 'funereal, secret, stern. Their solitude is desolation. They seem to stifle in their black gorges a story of sullen despair. No tender sentiment is nourished in their shade.' Even the mountain's names underscored this melancholy: Mount Misery, Mount Dreadful and Mount Despair.

But aside from an attachment to particular cities and countries there is a vocabulary of melancholy elements to be found in landscapes. Ruins are one such sign, whether they are the prosaic ruins of New Zealand and Australia: a dilapidated shop, a derelict barn, a chimney as an isolated sentinel; or the romantic cult of ruins, like those found in English landscapes, which have often been built as ruins, to suggest the passage of time, a tumbled temple; or the ruins of a past civilisation in the rainforest of South America. They all signal the mark of time's passage yet the endurance of the trace of things, in the rubble. Freud determined that melancholy differs from mourning in that it keeps the wound open. While a mourner, a griever, comes to a sense of closure and moves on, the melancholic embraces the condition of lingering. Ruins epitomise this condition, a prolonged and eternal ending. As architect Juhani Pallasmaa observes:

There is a strange melancholy in an abandoned home or a demolished apartment house that reveals traces and scars of intimate lives to the public gaze on its crumbling walls. It is touching to come across the remains of foundations or the hearth of a ruined or burnt house, half buried in the forest grass. The tenderness of the experience results from the fact that we do not imagine the house, but the home, life and faith of its members.[48]

Aligned with ruins are landscapes of death – cemeteries, memorials, sites of tragedy. Chapter 5 will explore some particular examples of such places, but at this point these landscapes can be drawn into this mapping of the place of melancholy. Like ruins, they evoke the passing of time, and particularly a sense of loss. Death circles the concept of melancholy, bearing with it both an individual and a collective melancholy. As Edgar Allan Poe reflected when beginning to write *The Raven*, 'of all melancholy topics what, according to the universal understanding of all mankind, is the most melancholy? Death was the obvious reply.'[49]

Liminal sites are also magnets for melancholy, pulling these sensations of loneliness and longing towards them. These are sites of passage from one realm into another – the land to the sky, and the land to the sea. Such marginal moments are found in Percy Bysshe Shelley's pause upon the 'wide and melancholy waste/Of putrid marshes'[50] or William Blake's 'melancholy shore',[51] a description which resonates with images in the vein of Edvard Munch's 'Melancholy' (1902) where the head-in-hands figure sits upon a gloomy beach. The ocean is a haunt of melancholy, and is allied with the god Saturn. Despite the assigning of 'earth' to melancholy in the humoral tradition, Saturn presides over water. And just as the need for infinitude impels the task of the collector, spaces of infinity also evoke melancholy. Staring at the vastness of the sky, at the expanse of ocean, or an endless road, elicits melancholy feelings associated with the conundrum of the limited nature of eternity. EM Cioran grappled with the loneliness of the place of melancholy, and he described how it was built upon the sensing of an interior and exterior feeling of infinity, and that the 'interior infinitude and vagueness of melancholy, not to be confused with the fecund infinity of love, demands a space whose borders are ungraspable… Melancholy detachment removes man from his natural surroundings. His outlook on infinity shows him to be lonely and forsaken. The sharper our consciousness of the world's infinity, the more acute our awareness of our own finitude.'[52]

The Time of Melancholy

The hunt for melancholy examines faces, places, and also the haunts of time. The feeling of age and time passing in the landscape is vital for melancholy's presence, and there are key times to look for melancholy. As suggested in the origins of humoral theory, particular diurnal and seasonal times are conducive to melancholy. Evening rather than morning, autumn rather than summer. Charles Baudelaire declares the ache of this moment, 'How poignant the late afternoons of autumn! Ah! Poignant to the verge of pain, for there are certain delicious sensations which are no less intense for being vague; and there is no sharper point than that of Infinity.'[53] The twelfth-century Japanese poet Jakuren offers a resonant meditation upon this moment, of day, of season, aligning it with the melancholy of solitude:

To be alone
It is of a color
That cannot be named:
This mountain where cedars rise
Into the autumn dusk.[54]

John Milton's *Il Penseroso* makes a plea to 'Hide me from Day's garish eie' and instead to inhabit the time of the nightingales, and seek the 'dimm religious light'. And melancholy persists through late afternoon, twilight, evening, and sometimes into night itself. Not the absolute darkness of night, but one which is moonlit, as the moon herself is the 'sovereign mistress of true melancholy',[55] that time when 'all the fowls/Are warmly housed, save bats and owls.'[56] These threshold times lead from a period of lightness – the sanguine – to the darker times beyond: liminal moments of passing from one time to another, times of evanescence and senescence, of fading and ageing.

As is typical with melancholy, the situation is circular – do such times *cause* melancholy, or are melancholy feelings *drawn towards* these times? Hippocrates traced psychic disturbances to certain seasonal changes, and melancholy was experienced during spring and autumn. The seasonal affects were also believed by some to be physiological. As Hugo de Folieto, a monastic theologian from around the twelfth century, wrote, black bile 'reigns in the left side of the body; its seat is the spleen; it is cold and dry. It makes men irascible, timid, sleepy or sometimes wakeful. It issues from the eyes. Its quantity increases in autumn.'[57]

In addition to this physiological cause, there are inherent qualities of the times which seem conducive to feelings of sorrow and poignancy. John Keats' *To Autumn,* with its reverence for 'the season of mists and mellow fruitfulness' traces out the fugitive qualities of this time of year. The imminence of winter, the ending of summer, brings a sense of loss that is intangible, the unassigned sadness that melancholy embodies. There is something of the circularity of this in Žižek's recounting of 'the old racist joke about Gypsies', that 'when it rains they are happy because they know that after rain there is always sunshine, and when the sun shines, they feel sad because they know that after the sunshine it will at some point rain.'[58]

There is a particular quality of light that infuses autumn with poignant, intangible qualities, as captured in Giorgio de Chirico's recollection of particular influences on his paintings, which included 'the melancholy of beautiful autumn days, afternoons in Italian cities'.[59] Poet Emily Dickinson finds melancholy light in winter, writing of the 'certain Slant of light' on winter afternoons 'That oppresses, like the Heft / of Cathedral Tunes – and When it comes –, the Landscape listens / Shadows – hold their breath / When it goes, 'tis like the Distance / On the look of Death –'[60]

The Chinese find melancholy in autumn, as it is the time of the commencement of Yin, or negative, energy, captured in the phrase, 'Moved by autumn, a zither musician contemplates the past'. A fusion of image and sound, this poetic fragment encapsulates the poignancy of autumn, as 'the music of the zither is desolate and heavy, like the thud of autumn fruits falling on the ground.'[61]

Autumn's associative power is strong. This liminal season, sitting at the edge of summer passing into winter, metaphorically evokes allusions to our own lives. For Hugues, the tormented hero of Georges Rodenbach's *Bruges-la-Morte*, it is October which suggests the melancholy metaphor of a dwindling life, and within it the poignant possibility of summer lingering, of his 'belated passion, sad October inflamed by a chance of late-blooming roses!'[62] And for the unnamed 'I' of Gustave Flaubert's novella, it is the eponymous *November* which encapsulates autumn, 'that melancholy season that suits memories so well. When the trees have lost their leaves, when the sky at sunset still preserves the russet hue that fills with gold the withered grass, it is sweet to watch the final fading of the fires that until recently burnt within you.'[63]

This sense of decay, of senescence, was experienced culturally for the Elizabethans, and their concern about the decay of the world itself was the origin of the 'metaphysical shudder'. Sir Thomas Browne captured this anxiety over the apparent futility of mankind, of the inevitable, imminent end to things, in his *Religio Medici*, the precursor to his funeral sermon *Urn Burial,* in a passage which speaks of how it is 'too late' to be ambitious, how too much has already passed away. Browne re-cast the Pyramids as 'mere pillars of snow'.[64] This is what George Williamson called the seventeenth century's 'melancholy of living in the afternoon of time'.[65]

So, in the wider sweep of history, as well as at the fleeting moments of autumn and twilight, melancholy intensifies at particular times. And the Renaissance is the prime time for the hunt – in the era known as Age of Melancholy. The seventeenth and eighteenth centuries were a high point for melancholia, when the unlikely bedfellows of science and art both circled around melancholy, prodding, poking, hypothesising. Medicine, metaphysics and drama, religion, architecture and poetry: all troubled themselves with the furthering of the understanding of melancholy, whether as disease, temperament or mood.

Early Modernity saw some of the key works on melancholy emerge, as a symptom of the age. The vanguard of the time is Timothy Bright's *Treatise of Melan-*

choly (1586), followed by Shakespeare's *Hamlet*, which was first performed in 1600, and Robert Burton's *The Anatomy of Melancholy* in 1621. Alongside these landmarks are the poetry of Milton's *Il Penseroso* (1632), and, moving into the eighteenth century, Alexander Pope's *Eloisa to Abelard,* with its 'deep solitudes and awful cells, /Where heav'nly-pensive contemplation dwells, /And ever-musing melancholy reigns' (1717). A key shift of this time was the move from the concern with discerning melancholy in individuals as with Bright and Burton, towards the lyrical melancholy of non-human subjects, in music, atmosphere and landscape.

Burton's 'love melancholy' became an icon of the age of the Romantics, as one of the key co-ordinates of the idea of 'sensibility'. As discussed in Chapter 1, melancholic sensibility was, for many, a feigned affectation, such was the desire to be associated with the connection between melancholy and literary genius. Yet, it was not a unisex melancholia that suffused the time. While, for a man, aspiring to melancholia was a noble and romantic pursuit, for women it was a lose-lose situation. As Elizabeth A Dolan notes, 'Romantic women poets ran the risk of being culturally disempowered by medical definitions of women's nervous illnesses or by an association with unfeminine reason.'[66] 'Melancholia' was diagnosed in men, but in women it was the 'vapours'. Sensibility became a male prerogative during the late eighteenth century, in efforts to divert it from being seen as irrational, with connotations of femininity, and Dolan argues that it was this development which moved melancholia out of the feminine domain in British Romanticism. Poet Charlotte Smith eluded this problem through a strategic sleight of hand, 'ventriloquizing' through the quotation of male poets, adopting their 'voice' – or even 'cross-dressing' – to draw melancholic content into her elegiac sonnets.[67] One of the voices Smith adopted was that of Werther – the hero of Johann Wolfgang von Goethe's *The Sorrows of Young Werther*. Melancholy was also the flavour of the moment in Germany, epitomised by Goethe's 'Young Werther', who was possessed with love melancholy, obsessed with death, and ultimately committed suicide.

As well as love melancholy, the heightened subjectivity of the age is also expressed in feelings for nature, and the sadness that is immanent in one's surroundings. The beauty of loneliness and isolation is central to this time, and the eighteenth-century Swiss writer Johann Georg Zimmerman described how this 'sort of sweet melancholy overcomes us in the lap of rural tranquillity when viewing all of nature's beauty [and]... solitude on occasion, but of course not always, transforms deep despondency into sweet melancholy.'[68] And the German Idealist, Friedrich Wilhelm Joseph von Schelling wrote in his *Weltalter*, or 'World Age', of the 'veil of melancholy which is spread over the whole of nature, the deep indestructible melancholy of all life'. The yearning for the infinite impels this sense of melancholy, the 'unappeasable grief' of the universe.[69]

As modernity develops through the rise of industrialisation and progress, it is a different melancholy that is the object of the hunt. Not the spirited melancholy of the Romantics, nor that of an affective relationship with Nature, nor the ornamental melancholy adopted by the aristocracy as a decoration for their souls; here it is a bleak sensibility borne of the individual's place in the world –

a sense of abandonment. Dislocation and detachment emerges at all levels, from the individual to society at large in the face of, as Washington Irving termed it, 'the melancholy progress of improvement',[70] or as EM Cioran remarked of the West, 'Machines and effort and that galloping melancholy – the West's last spasm.'[71] The Kantian Sublime, Hegelian 'alienation' and Kierkegaard's 'dread' all circle about this schism in the connection of self to space, and are all inflected with degrees of melancholy.

The emergence of 'self' and 'other' – or selfhood and alterity – as the underpinnings of human existence manifested the disconnection of the individual from the broader cultural setting. Yet this is a solitude which does not have the 'sweet melancholy' of Zimmerman, but more a 'bleak melancholy' which is inflicted rather than sought out. It is within this context, this cleaving, that modern psychoanalytical thought begins to develop and, with it, the Freudian notion of melancholy. Psychoanalysis gave a new lease of life to melancholy, adding to its conceptual framework, and expanding it as a mode of relating to experience and place.

Freudian psychoanalysis represents a further particularly intense time period of attention to melancholy. Through his hypothesis of the difference between melancholy and mourning, Freud circled back to the problematic conundrums which have always been present. Freud's landmark essay was *Mourning and Melancholia* in which he distinguished a sense of normal grief as mourning from abnormal grief as the pathological condition of melancholia. In mourning, or grieving, the self (or 'ego') 'gets over' whatever is lost but, with melancholia, 'the wound is kept open'. The consequences of this are that, while mourners move on to reclaim their lives, melancholics refract the pain back onto themselves: 'In mourning the world has become poor and empty; in melancholia it is the ego that has become so.'[72] Within this distinction Freud focused the panoptic thinking of the preceding millennia into a tight, synoptic kernel, and marked the zeitgeist of the new age of melancholia. The very idea of abnormality underscores such problematic contemporary dimensions of melancholy, seen in its interface with psychology and psychiatry, as demonstrated in the discussion of the DSM – the Diagnostic and Statistical Manual – in Chapter 1.

Freud's work in turn influenced the generation of psychoanalysts to follow, including Melanie Klein, Hannah Segal, Jacques Lacan and Julia Kristeva. Distinctive in this period of work on psychoanalysis is the broad cultural dimension to their work, of the shuttling between individual and society. The nihilism of modernity is intensely melancholy, and in Freudian terms, Western culture collectively experiences the pathological distress of the lost object, and 'normal mourning' fails. For cultures, the losses were elusively metaphysical – ideas like 'truth' that had formerly been found in philosophy and art were undone, questioned, taken away, leading to the feeling of abandonment and grief for the past. The art and literature born of such a predicament can be introspective and abjective, as, for example, in the work of the surrealists. Here, amidst landscapes of alienation, mystery, ruin, the crisis of modernity manifests itself sometimes as a vacuum, or sense of absence, and sometimes in unnerving hybrids and fusions where the familiar is made strange. René Magritte, Salvador Dali, and Giorgio de Chirico exemplify the disturbing visions of the art of this melancholic age.

The sense of abandonment and rupture as the marks of modernity's machine of progress are embedded within the experience of individual cultures. Claude Lévi-Strauss's anthropological study of dying non-Western cultures in the early twentieth century, *Tristes Tropiques,* describes his encounters in a range of settings, mainly within Brazil. There is a strong feeling of longing in his writing, and the very title of the work has been considered untranslatable, as it does not simply mean the 'sad tropics,' but embodies melancholic yearning for these passing cultures. One of the passages from his book, a page from his field notes, expresses this 'dreamy melancholy', or, in the Weightmans' translation, 'brooding melancholy', where he describes his impressions of camping with the Nambikwara, and 'anguish and pity at human beings so bereft; some relentless cataclysm seems to have crushed them against the ground in a hostile land, leaving them naked and shivering by their flickering fires.'[73] Lévi-Strauss was defending the Nambikwara against more maudlin descriptions, and he emphasised instead their 'immense Kindness ... And something which might be called the most truthful and moving expression of human love.'[74]

Susan Sontag saw Lévi-Strauss's *Tristes Tropiques* as an exemplary work which captures all the poignancy of the crumbling history, laced with doubts, and requiring a 'profound detachment'. She described how 'the anthropologist is not only the mourner of the cold world of primitives, but its custodian as well. Lamenting among the shadows, struggling to distinguish the archaic from the pseudo-archaic, he acts out a heroic, diligent, and complex modern pessimism.'[75]

The melancholy of progress and culture at large also infuses the work of philosophers Søren Kierkegaard, Friedrich Nietzsche and Walter Benjamin, and poets and writers like Charles Baudelaire and Fyodor Dostoevsky. Progress was a double-edge sword, bringing not only the promise of material wealth, but also a pervasive sense of estrangement. This accelerated through the twentieth century, with increasing deprivation and social isolation. Even amongst the wealthy, the ever more introspective modes of entertainment, the personal music players, television, and cellphones, meant that the emphasis put on the individual's own bubble of existence had a deleterious effect on interpersonal relationships. The individualised spheres of existence eroded the greater connectivity of communities, and limited the possibilities for authentic interaction. Added to this are the pressures of globalisation. For all the promise of the 'global village', there is instead more of a ghost town. Melancholy is, as Harvie Ferguson put it in his examination of Kierkegaard, 'the empty depth of modernity'.[76]

Modernity also brought about the particular species, 'Left Melancholy', or in its native German, '*linke Melancholie*'. Developed early in the twentieth century by Walter Benjamin, the term originally expressed a type of narcissism. Although Benjamin was one of the pre-eminent philosophers of melancholy, excavating its richness and contradictions, in 'Left Melancholy' he cast it as a form of criticism. The inertia that comes with melancholy, the wanting to resist closure, to prolong or retard things, in political terms becomes in-activism: a 'mournful, conservative, backward-looking attachment to a feeling, analysis, or relationship that has been rendered thing-like and frozen in the heart of the putative leftist.'[77] 'Left Melancholy' became significant during what was known as the 'German Autumn' – 1977-1981 – a time of terrorism, murders and hijackings when left-leaning intellectuals found themselves in a state of paralysis. Consumed by a pressing cultural pessimism, an existential crisis of sorts, a feeling of abandonment, they entered a state of melancholy detachment. Wolf Lepenies describes such a position as 'retreatist', where there is neither the will to conform, nor the oppositional force to rebel ... instead there is a move to stand apart, in melancholy mode. In literary form, 'Left Melancholy' underlies works in the vein of Günter Grass's *From the Diary of a Snail*, which explicitly uses the emblem of Dürer's *Melencolia I* to evoke the certain brooding quality of this detachment. Grass delivered a lecture in 1971 where he described melancholy as a 'substitute for action', and this stagnation is amplified in the summation that, 'What is dangerous about the gaze of the melancholic is that it causes life (time) to flow out of objects – it petrifies them... one of the forgotten symbols of melancholy Walter Benjamin... reminds us, is stone.'[78]

Melancholic inertia also afflicts twentieth-century refugees, displaced and alienated from their homelands. Svetlana Boym describes how the landscapes of collective memory can have a reflective nostalgia and, with this, a combination of both mourning – of a 'normal' grief for the losses of the past – and also of melancholia. The disconnection with their landscapes eats at the individual and the collective, since it is within landscapes that we find a sense of home and identity. To be removed from such landscapes, or to have them removed through war or other catastrophes, induces mourning and melancholia, and loss which can only be partially recalled, as part of the 'labor of grief'.[79]

The early twenty-first century is another era of melancholic intensity, a good time for the hunt. While the Romantic era was a time of lyrical melancholy, and modernity introduced themes of *ennui* and the struggle for selfhood, here in late modernity it gathers further dimensions. The pressures of consumerist-driven imperatives, with their seemingly endless array of goals, increase daily. The expanding culture of happiness, with its efforts to eliminate sadness, instead has the opposite effect, by raising expectations that continual happiness is something to strive for and undermining the role sadness has in the human condition.

This new *Age of Melancholy*[80], as encountered in Chapter 1, is a troubled one. That is nothing new in the legacy of this paradoxical concept, but the contemporary age of melancholy is torn in different directions. Is the increase in melancholy an authentic response to the pressures of contemporary existence, where it might be considered a pervasive mood? Or is it an aberration resulting from a change in the scientific definitions of mental illness? These debates will continue for the time to come, as science and art, and all of the grey space between, continue their tug of war. Melancholy, however, has many allies, and Chapter 3 explores some of the associated concepts which bring added richness to the beauty of sadness.

Notes

1. EM Cioran, *On the Heights of Despair*, p.41.
2. Frances A Yates, *The Occult Philosophy in the Elizabethan Age*, p.51.
3. Jean-Luc Marion, *God Without Being*, p.132.
4. Jean Clair, 'Saturn's Museum', p.32.
5. Jeffrey K Aronson and Manoj Ramachandran, 'The diagnosis of art: melancholy and the Portrait of Dr Gachet'.
6. Raymond Klibansky, Erwin Panofsky and Fritz Saxl, *Saturn and Melancholy: Studies in the History of Natural Philosophy, Religion and Art*, p.287.
7. Naomi E. Maurer, *The Pursuit of Spiritual Wisdom: The Thought and Art of Vincent Van Gogh*, p.109.
8. Jean-Etienne-Dominque Esquirol (1845). *Mental Maladies: A Treatise on Insanity*. Cited in Christine Ross, *The Aesthetics of Disengagement: Contemporary Art and Depression*, p.6.
9. Klibansky, Panofsky and Saxl, *Saturn and Melancholy*, p.319.
10. William Shakespeare, *Hamlet*, Act 1 Scene 2, lines 77–84, p.112.
11. Aris Sarafianos, 'The many colours of black bile: the melancholies of knowing and feeling', pp.1–17, passim.
12. 'With a green and yellow melancholy/She sat like patience on a monument', William Shakespeare, *Twelfth Night, or What You Will*, p.28.
13. EM Cioran, *Tears and Saints*, p.43.
14. HS Akiskal and KK Akiskal, 'A mixed state core for melancholia: an exploration in history, art and clinical science', p.45.
15. See Frances A Yates, *The Occult Philosophy in the Elizabethan Age*.
16. Thomas Gray (1742) cited in Leigh Hunt, *A Book for a Corner, Or, Selections in Prose and Verse from Authors*, p.118 (*ça ne laisse que de s'amuser* is translated in Leigh Hunt as 'does nothing but trifle').
17. Frances A Yates, *The Occult Philosophy in the Elizabethan Age*, p.51.
18. Gaston Bachelard, *The Poetics of Reverie*, p.64.
19. ibid, p.12.
20. William Shakespeare, *Four Comedies ('As You Like It')*, p.479.
21. A fascinating discussion of the melancholy nature of art history can be found in *The Art Bulletin*, March 2007.
22. Jean Clair, 'Saturn's Museum', p.40.
23. Jean Baudrillard quoted in Peter Schwenger, *The Tears of Things:*

Melancholy and Physical Objects, p.85.

24. Susan Sontag, *The Volcano Lover*, p.24.

25. Tacita Dean, *Tacita Dean*, p.76.

26. Sisyphus, an ancient Greek, was given the punishment of rolling a rock to the top of the hill, only to watch it roll down again and then complete the task, for all of eternity. Albert Camus' *The Myth of the Sisyphus* conveys the anguish of this predicament, 'Again I fancy Sisyphus returning toward his rock, and the sorrow was in the beginning. When the images of earth cling too tightly to memory, when the call of happiness becomes too insistent, it happens that melancholy rises in man's heart: this is the rock's victory, this is the rock itself. The boundless grief is too heavy to bear.' Albert Camus, *The Myth of the Sisyphus*, p.122.

27. WG Sebald, *The Rings of Saturn*, p.283.

28. Klibansky, Panofsky and Saxl, *Saturn and Melancholy*, p.235.

29. WG Sebald, *Vertigo*, p.212.

30. Italo Calvino, *Six Memos for the New Millennium*, pp.19–20.

31. Kerry O'Brien, *Mime Artist Bows Out*.

32. Søren Kierkegaard, *Either/Or: A Fragment of Life*, p.49.

33. Christine Ross, *The Aesthetics of Disengagement: Contemporary Art and Depression*, p.40.

34. Roger Caillois, 'Mimicry and Legendary Psychasthenia', p.25.

35. John Evelyn (1641) cited in EF Carrick, *A Calendar of British Taste from 1600 to 1800,* p.38.

36. ibid, p.50.

37. ibid, p.103.

38. ibid, p.170.

39. Orhan Pamuk, *Istanbul: Memories of a City*, p.89.

40. Iain Sinclair, *Lights out for the Territory: 9 Excursions in the Secret History of London*, p.91.

41. Peter Ackroyd, *Hawksmoor*.

42. William Butler Yeats, *Letters to Katharine Tynan*, p.62.

43. Joseph Addison (1712) cited in EF Carrick, *A Calendar of British Taste from 1600 to 1800*, p.164.

44. Natalia Ginzburg, *The Little Virtues*, p.21.

45. Sam Neill and Judy Rymer, *Cinema of Unease: A Personal Journey*.

46. Martin Edmond, 'The Abandoned House as a Refuge for the

Imagination', p.154.

47. Marcus Clarke (c.1870) in Bill Wannan, *The Australian: Yarns, Ballads, Legends, Traditions of the Australian People*, p.225.

48. Juhani Pallasmaa, 'Identity, Domicile and Identity: Notes on the Phenomenology of Home'.

49. Edgar Allan Poe from *The Philosophy of Composition*, cited in Orhan Pamuk, *Istanbul: Memories of a City*, pp.101–102.

50. Percy Bysshe Shelley, 'Alastor: Or, the Spirit of Solitude' in *The Major Works*, p.100.

51. William Blake (1783), 'King Edward the Third' in David V Erdman (ed), *The Complete Poetry and Prose of William Blake*, p.437.

52. EM Cioran, *On the Heights of Despair*, p.30.

53. Charles Baudelaire, *Paris Spleen*, p.8.

54. Jakuren in Andrew Juniper, *Wabi-Sabi: The Japanese Art of Impermanence*, p.76.

55. William Shakespeare (1606) 'Antony and Cleopatra' cited in EF Carrick, *A Calendar of British Taste from 1600 to 1800*, p.8.

56. ibid, p.24.

57. Klibansky, Panofsky and Saxl, p.108.

58. Slavoj Žižek, *Melancholy and the Critical Act*, pp.661–662.

59. Giorgio de Chirico, *The Memoires of Giorgio de Chirico*, p.61.

60. Emily Dickinson (c.1861). 'There's a certain Slant of light' (Poem 258) in Wendy Martin, *The Cambridge Introduction to Emily Dickinson*, p.95.

61. Zhengdao Ye, *An inquiry into sadness in Chinese*, p.370.

62. Georges Rodenbach, *Bruges-la-Morte*, p.85.

63. Gustave Flaubert, *November*, p.3.

64. Thomas Browne quoted in George Williamson, *Mutability, Decay, and Seventeenth-Century Melancholy*, p.148.

65. ibid.

66. Elizabeth A Dolan, 'British Romantic melancholia: Charlotte Smith's *Elegiac Sonnets,* medical discourse and the problem of sensibility', p.238.

67. ibid, p.248.

68. Johann Georg Zimmerman (1796) *Solitude Considered*, cited in Wolf Lepenies, *Melancholy and Society*, p.64.

69. David L Clark, 'Heidegger's Craving: Being-on-Schelling', p.14.

70. From *Thoughts of a Hermit,* 1815 quoted in Edward J Nygren, *Views and Visions: American Landscapes before 1830*, p.58.

71. EM Cioran, *All Gall is Divided*, p.56.

72. Sigmund Freud, *On Murder, Mourning and Melancholia*, pp.205-206.

73. Claude Lévi-Strauss, *Tristes Tropiques*, p.293.

74. ibid.

75. Susan Sontag, *Against Interpretation, and Other Essays*, p.81.

76. Harvie Ferguson, *Melancholy and the Critique of Modernity: Søren Kierkegaard's Religious Psychology*, p.35.

77. Wendy Brown, 'Resisting Left Melancholy', p.22.

78. Paula Salvio cited in Marla Morris, *Curriculum and the Holocaust: Competing Sites of Memory and Representation*, p.185.

79. Svetlana Boym, *The Future of Nostalgia*, p.55.

80. Dan G Blazer, *The Age of Melancholy: 'Major Depression' and its Social Origins*.

Acedia, Anomie, et al.:
Melancholy's Allies

Laurence Aberhart, *Verdun, France, 25 October 1994*

3

Acedia, Anomie, et al.:
Melancholy's Allies

Melancholy… melancholy? Or is it toothache?
Werner Herzog, *Where the Green Ants Dream*[1]

Melancholy's complexity is reflected in the many allied terms which hover around it, or are subsumed within it. Each of these contains certain dimensions of melancholy, and contributes to the richness of the melancholy constellation. The ideas outlined below, in alphabetic order, are all melancholy in part. In some cases they share emotional connections, or they might be subsets of the vast domain of melancholy. The family resemblances are occasionally so strong that they might be used interchangeably with melancholy in some situations. The terms are intermeshed and overlaid in a complex mix of contexts, and only a brief summary is possible here.

Acedia

The melancholy of boredom, *acedia*, grew out of the *taedium vitae* of ancient times, the *ennui* of world weariness and despair at life's tedium. The need to escape from *taedium vitae* was one of the few permissible reasons for suicide amongst the Romans, recognising the burden of such an emotion. *Taedium vitae* affected both the body and the mind. The soul's illness was manifested somatically, in physical unwellness. On the tomb of the Roman Marcus Pomponius Bassulus is an inscription which explains his suicide as a consequence of this physical and psychical affliction: 'But vexed of anxieties of a hard-pressed mind as well as by numerous pains of the body, so that both were extremely disgusting, I procured for myself the death I wished for.'[2]

During the Dark Ages, in the time of the Desert Fathers – the monks that were stationed in the deserts of Egypt – *acedia* was identified as a spiritual illness. The rigours of asceticism and devotion to prayer made for a very disciplined and isolated life. Living as hermits, they were required to rise at 4am for prayers, and to spend their days in solitude. Evagrius Ponticus, one of the desert monks based in the Desert of Cells, was conflicted over his occasional reluctance to carry out these rigorous and disciplined tasks, and was dogged by a sense of lassitude and psychic exhaustion. In the fourth century John Chrysostom described the plight of a monk suffering from monastic melancholy, with the symptoms of 'terrifying nightmares, speech disorders, fits, faints, unjustified feelings of hopelessness about his salvation, and being tormented by a prompting to commit suicide.'[3]

Another of the Desert Fathers, John Cassian, described 'accidie' as the 'midday' or 'noonday demon' (or the 'sixth' hour as it was to monks), the time when tiredness and heat were at their most intense, manifesting themselves in restlessness, a sense of time dragging, loneliness and idleness. Psalm 91:6 warns against the 'destruction that wasteth at noonday'.[4] Cures were perseverance, courage, or the redoubling of efforts at prayer, all targeted towards increased spiritual fortitude. But St Jerome suggested that *acedia* needed 'Hippocratic treatments', meaning that he saw it as a physical illness rather than a spiritual one. And in recent times *acedia* is glossed as 'depression' in some translations of these passages from the Dark Ages, offering a retrospective diagnosis of monastic lassitude.

The connection between *acedia* and the religious community was reinforced by its definition as a sin. In early Christian times it was listed in the seven deadly sins as the sin of Sadness, where the apathy and lack of joy were interpreted as the refusal to embrace the goodness of spirituality and appreciation of God. The fact that *acedia* was a sin against God, of not loving him, of being repelled by divine goodness, made it particularly troublesome. *Acedia* was on and off the list of sins, or chief vices, at different times, sitting alongside gluttony, fornication, covetousness, anger, dejection, vainglory and pride. In the ancient hermeneutic tradition it was seen as one of the most lethal vices – 'the only one for which no pardon was possible.'[5]

Acedia originally encompassed both sadness and lassitude, or more precisely what Jackson describes as two triads: sorrow-dejection-despair and neglect-idleness-indolence.[6] *Acedia* was originally used interchangeably with another term, *tristitia* (see entry below). Over time *acedia* took on the negative connotations of despondency, and *tristitia* the positive ones of noble suffering. While *acedia* was considered a consequence of monastic life, a kind of occupational hazard, it later became more widely recognised. During the more secular times of the Renaissance, the lassitude and lethargy of *acedia* were thought to be caused by a humoral imbalance, either phlegmatic or melancholy, and it was therefore seen not as a sin but a disease.

Sloth and laziness persisted as an auxiliary component of melancholy, and became associated with the 'great ennui' of modernity, what Schopenhauer saw as the corrosive force of the modern age. This return to the ancient's sense of *taedium vitae* appears in Cheyne's writings on the 'English malady', where he identified Luxury and Laziness as the causes of the growth in nervous disorders, particularly melancholia (see Chapter 4).

Anomie/Anomy

Related to *acedia*'s melancholic reaction against life's strictures, anomie is a modern form of alienation from the world. The isolation of anomie stems from a sense of displacement, whether being literally removed from one's home, or from feeling unconnected to the placelessness of contemporary existence. Early twentieth-century sociological theorist Emile Durkheim related the anxiousness of anomie to the individual's feeling of failure in the face of society's expectations, what he called a 'normlessness' in that individuals couldn't reach what were perceived as norms.

Throughout the twentieth century the plight of the anomic has escalated with the increasing levels of affluence, acutely captured in the term 'affluenza', defined as 'a painful, contagious, socially transmitted condition of overload, debt, anxiety and waste.'[7] Individuals manipulated by advertising into the need to have material goods, to achieve a particular status and so on, are driven towards the melancholic anomie of feeling alienated and displaced from a world beyond their means. Implicated in this is the 'culture of happiness', the expectation that, with sufficient investment, it is possible to bypass anything which might make us feel sad. However, this simply adds to the anomie. In his commentary on the exhibition *Mélancolie: Genie et Folie en Occident,* historian Georges Minois pointed out the predicament of a 'society of consumption and imme-diate satisfaction' full of 'compulsively happy people', who feel obliged to be 'optimists by command'.[8] He suggests that this pursuit of happiness is in fact disabling, where the constant striving for a flawless existence has the opposite effect, making people vulnerable to the 'demo-cratic form of melancholy' – depression. Anomie as affluenza is what Hamilton and Denniss call 'luxury fever'.[9] It is the flipside to Cheyne's connection between luxury and laziness, as here it is the unrequited desire for luxury, rather than its numbing excesses, which is the seat of melancholy.

Et in Arcadia Ego

Although an actual existing place in Greece, in the con-text of the iconic phrase *Et in Arcadia Ego,* Arcadia is a mythical paradise, the setting for Roman poet Virgil's bucolic sequence, the *Eclogues.* A rural idyll and extension of the vision of a Golden Age, Arcadia represents a place of untrammelled happiness and peaceful existence, a pleasant past time. It is the root of the love of pastoral imagery, of scenes of nature gently modified by culture, and of the associations of such settings with the ideals of Utopia. For this reason the ideas of Arcadia were borne around the world by those in search of a perfect life, an ideal existence.

Given such an idyllic pedigree, how then does the

phrase *Et in Arcadia Ego* – 'even in Arcadia I am' – have connotations of melancholy? The phrase and its grammar have been widely debated over the centuries, including speculation on who the 'I', the *ego*, is. Some interpretations have nostalgic connotations, suggesting that it is a phrase reminiscing about a bygone age. Art historian Erwin Panofsky's seminal study of the phrase rests on two key translations, the sentimental elegy of 'I, too, lived in Arcadia', or the more brooding lament, 'Death is even in Arcadia'.[10]

In Nicholas Poussin's iconic painting of the *Et in Arcadia Ego* theme (1637-1638), a group of classical shepherds are in deep contemplation of a tomb on which the phrase is written, one tracing the words with his finger. The tomb, and the hint of death's presence, lend weight to this haunting of Arcadia. It therefore becomes another of the paradoxes that are embedded in ideas associated with melancholy, the contradiction between the beauty of paradise, and the presence of death. As a *memento mori*, or reminder of death, the tradition of *Et in Arcadia Ego* expresses the melancholy relationship with time, with the transience of things. In his study of the two images painted by Poussin on the theme, Anthony Blunt summarises the thematic content as, in the first, 'regret and disillusionment at the transitoriness of life' and, in the second, the additional component of 'resignation'.[11]

The *Et in Arcadia Ego* theme became a frame for the encounters of Western explorers with the South Pacific. Like Claude Lévi-Strauss, with his conflicted melancholy over his time spent in the tropics, as expressed in *Tristes Tropiques*, eighteenth-century explorers visiting the South Seas isles, including Tahiti and Fiji, were also distracted by a certain poignancy in these archetypical paradises. Sydney Parkinson, an artist who travelled on Captain James Cook's voyages, exemplified the practice of depicting Arcadian scenes, peopled with noble savages. Places like Tahiti confounded the visitors from Europe, as, on one hand, there were quite evidently the signs that a Golden Age had existed in this setting of tropical abundance and pleasant scenery. Against this, though, were disturbing aspects, including behaviour that seemed immoral to the eyes of the explorers, and strange funerary practices. Parkinson painted a funerary setting in Tahiti, including the presence of a chest with an offering on it, a funerary structure, and mourning figures. When William Woollett made an engraving based on Parkinson's 1770 wash drawing, *View in the Island of Huaheine with an Ewhara and a small altar with an offering on it,* he endowed it with 'melancholy grandeur'.[12] The offering to the dead and the mourning figures were aspects which were emphasised in the image, and the exoticness of the paradisiacal setting was intensified. Here is a prime example of *Et in Arcadia Ego,* a reminder of the presence of Death, even in these far-flung isles.

Lacrimae Rerum

Lacrimae Rerum is a phrase which comes from Virgil's *Aeneid,* line 462 of Book 1. Aeneas, the *Aeneid*'s central character, finds tears falling while he contemplates murals showing the battles of the Trojan War. Faced with the images of the dead in war he is affected by the sense of life's futility, of the passing of things, and utters the line *sunt lacrimae rerum et mentem mortalia tangent,* 'there are tears for misfortune and mortal sorrows touch the heart'.[13]

Translations vary, and the phrase sometimes appears in English as 'tears *for* things', and sometimes as 'tears *of* things'. This subtle shift in preposition opens up two melancholy connections. In the first, the tears *for* things are, in the Virgilian sense, for the way in which the reminders of mortality touch the soul, for the human condition itself. While Aeneas's tears were for the things he looked upon, there is an inverse of this, which bestows an affective melancholy on what is observed – the tears *of* things. As Peter Schwenger explains, although the use of 'of' might be stretching Classical grammar, the interpretation 'the tears of things' conveys the melancholy inherent in objects. Moreover, Schwenger illuminates the word *rerum*, which is often glossed as 'the affairs of men' or 'events' (perhaps because Aeneas was observing tableaux of the human dimension of war), but actually means 'things', as in Lucretius's *de rerum natura*: 'on the nature of things'.

Love Melancholy

In his *Anatomy of Melancholy*, Robert Burton devoted an entire section to 'Love Melancholy'. He offered that the 'last and best' cure for love melancholy is to let those afflicted have their desire. But, for a true melancholic, closure is not the point. And, of course, the impossibility of closure, of being allowed to prolong one's desire, is the critical part of love melancholy. To have desire fulfilled is to lose that very thing, as the longing is no longer. Love melancholy keeps its wound open, dwells upon unrequitedness, feeds upon it. Love-sickness, insane love, and erotomania, are terms used to describe the various species of love melancholy – that condition of despair and desperation. As Avicenna described it in his tenth-century *Canon of Medicine*, love is an illness which is 'a form of mental distress similar to melancholia in which man's mind is excitedly and continuously preoccupied with beauty itself and with the forms and signs thereof.'[14]

Love melancholy enlists both the god of love, Eros, and the god of death, Thanatos. While Eros deals with desire, Thanatos maintains the sense of impending loss associated with the death of things, with the end of love. The two are constantly at play, Eros and Thanatos do-si-do, circling around and around. This dance of love and death is sometimes extended to the ending of life as an extreme escape from the unbearable plight of unrequited love. The suicide of Goethe's Young Werther represents such an escape, and he describes it as a sacrifice. His farewell letters to the focus of his desire, Lotte, plot this trajectory of love and death, heading towards this ultimate expression of love melancholy. For Werther, suicide represents the eternity of love, a way to ensure it will not end, telling Lotte that when she also dies he will fly to her and be with her 'in eternal embrace, in the presence of the Almighty'.[15] There is a certain honour associated with those who declare they will die for love. Marie-Henri Beyle, the nineteenth-century writer known as Stendhal, wrote at length on love and, in his *Fragments*, he advised, 'True love makes the thought of death frequent, easy, without terrors; it merely becomes the standard of comparison, the price one would pay for many things.'[16]

The goddess Hera is also implicated in love melancholy, in the love-sickness known as *amor hereos*, or *ereos*. The idea of *amor hereos* is what is sometimes called the 'domi-

nant love' of Hera, who became jealous over Zeus's affair
with the nymph Io – her own priestess. But the interpretations of *hereos* are not straightforward. It is an ambiguous word and some sources elide it to *eros* or even to
heroes' love. One of the key uses of the phrase is in
Chaucer's *Knight's Tale* in describing the sorrows of Arcite:

> His speche nor his vois, though men it herde.
> And in his gere, for al the world he ferde
> Nat oonly lyk the loveres maladye
> Of Hereos, but rather lyk manye
> Engendred of humour malencolyk,
> Biforen, in his celle fantastyk.[17]

This *amor hereos* is specifically associated with melancholy
in the writings of the Middle Ages, and physicians of the
time would concern themselves with this type of love-
sickness. John of Tornamira was the physician to the popes
in the fifteenth century, and in his discussion 'de melan-
colia' he explains *amor hereos* and relates it to the dryness
of the brain. The idea of *amor hereos* is also part of Robert
Burton's work, where he uses the phrase 'Heroical or
Love-Melancholy'. Although this is often interpreted as
the love melancholy of heroes, knights and nobles, Burton
makes direct reference to the lineage of physicians who
used it in the sense of 'hereos'. Concluding his 57-page article plotting the idea of *amor hereos* through the ages, John
Livingstone Lowe declares that he has done his dash, but
that, 'As a chapter in the history of psychiatry; as part of the
texture of forgotten modes of thought; as a curious light
upon dark places, the lore of the lover's malady has a vivid
and enduring human interest.'[18]

Nostalgia

Nostalgia holds a particular affinity with melancholy. Like melancholy, nostalgia was also considered an illness, the disease of homesickness. Johannes Hofer, a Swiss medical student, invented the word in the late seventeenth century, as a hybrid of the Greek words for returning home (*nostos*) and pain or longing (*algos*). Despite its construction, Hofer's 'nostalgia' meant not the pain of returning home, but the anguish of being away, of being apart from one's place in the world. He developed the word as a diagnosis of unwellness detected amongst Swiss mercenaries who spent long periods away from home, with the symptoms including 'persistent thoughts about home, melancholy, insomnia, anorexia, weakness, anxiety, lack of breath, and palpitations of the heart'.[19]

And, like melancholy, it has been dissected by physicians in search of its pathology but in recent times has become categorised as an emotion rather than a physical ailment. It is also, like melancholy, notoriously slippery. As Svetlana Boym puts it, '[n]ostalgia remains unsystematic and unsynthesizable; it seduces rather than convinces'.[20] In *The Art of Memory*, Frances Yates makes the connection between melancholia and memory, noting that melancholics are best able to retain memory 'owing to their hard and dry constitution'.[21] The medieval philosopher and theologian Albertus Magnus explained that, based upon the theory of the four humours, melancholy could produce good memories 'because the melancholic received the impressions of images more firmly and retained them longer than persons of other temperaments'.[22] It is not an ordinary 'dry-cold' melancholy which is associated with memory, and specifically 'the temperament of *reminiscibilitas*', or reminiscence, but a 'dry-hot' melancholy, intellectual and inspired.

With parallels in the French *mal du pays* (country sickness) and the German *Heimweh* (home-pain), nostalgia is a form of bitter-sweetness, a love of longing, a joyous pain. Like lovesickness's embracing of the agonies of unrequited love, homesickness revels in the impossibility of returning to a particular moment. The impossibility of actually returning to the past, a lost object which most certainly cannot be regained, casts nostalgia as melancholy *par excellence*. Nostalgia is a melancholic prolonging, a retardation of closure – nostalgics do not seek a cure, they want the pleasure of the pain of separation. After all, as Immanuel Kant advised, the *Heimkunft*, or homecoming, is often 'very disappointing' because in the intervening time that very place may have been 'wholly transformed' – to return to that exact place is impossible.[23] In echoing melancholy's fixation on a single object, nostalgia's obsession with a particular time and place is able to block out all connection to the present. This impossibility allows the moment to persist untrammelled amidst the contemporary. For this reason nostalgia is often seen as a reaction to progress, a yearning for simpler times, a longing for that which has been sacrificed.

Nostalgia's sentimentalising is also a process of editing. In yearning for that which has past, only the positive aspects are recalled, amplified, valorised, while the negative dimensions of that previous time fly under the radar. Places are often fragmentary, discontinuous, as in poet Rainer Maria Rilke's reverie on how a remembered house is 'not a building, but is quite dissolved and distributed inside me; here one room, there another, and here a bit of corridor which, however, does not connect the two rooms, but is conserved in me in fragmentary form. Thus the whole thing is scattered about inside me, the rooms, the stairs that descended with such ceremonious slowness, others, narrow cages that mounted in a spiral movement, in the darkness of which we advanced like the blood in our veins.'[24]

As part of nostalgia's editing of place and time there is an element of imaginative invention, of wistful reconstruction. Things which may have been negative in the past can cross over into a positive recollection, so that memories even of war can be suffused with a golden glow. The deprivations of Communist East Germany fade in the face of a species of nostalgia called *ostalgie*, a hybrid of the German *Ost* (east) and *nostalgie*. The pre-1989 reunification abbreviation of the DDR, the *Deutsche Demokratische Republik* or German Democratic Republic, is now a sought-after emblem on t-shirts and other memorabilia. And it is not just those who experienced the communist regime that seek these items. One of the curious things about nostalgia is that it sometimes involves borrowing the memories of others. Just like the DDR emblem, CCCP – the Russian form of the former USSR – is also in vogue around the world. And the imagery of the hammer and sickle printed on a t-shirt is nostalgically worn in the USA, for example, with all recollections of the schism of the Cold War conveniently consigned to the rubble of memory.

Refugees are perhaps the most poignant sufferers of nostalgia. Displaced from their homelands, refugees' memories of place gain even greater significance. Rather than the luxurious borrowing of the memories of others, or of looking back at leisure, the fragments of a former existence are bearers of identity, of a seat of one's self, for the nostalgic refugee. Nostalgia can take on a role of recovery in such settings – in both senses of the word – of aiding healing and of reclaiming that which is lost.

Pathos

Pathos resonates with one particular dimension of melancholy – that of suffering. As a means of intensifying or highlighting the presence of sadness and sorrow, pathos is a form of persuasion, and is found in any context in which this is an important task. For example, the persuasive power of pathos might be found in literature and art, but also in advertising and journalism. The use of stock tropes of pathos, shorthand for 'here is an example of suffering', can be found throughout all of these realms.

The quotidian pathos of news journalism and advertising places images of suffering in front of us daily. Embedded within many of these images is an evocation of melancholy, yet it is one which must be constantly renewed, and intensified, as our saturation with imagery and words progressively dulls their effectiveness. War photojournalism, advertising appeals for aid organisations, stories about local human tragedies, all enlist pathos in conveying their content. The deployment of pathos in advertising is often the most transparent, using direct appeals to sympathy and pity. The pathetic images of a starving child or an ill-treated animal are familiar examples of such techniques.

Taken to an extreme, pathos can undo melancholy. Pathos easily descends into parody and melodrama, becoming overly sentimentalised and drowning in emotion, and bathetic rather than pathetic. In this sense it can even become comedic, as bathos occurs when emotion becomes overwrought and instead undoes itself through overstatement. Pathos can also, as in the case of the 'society of the spectacle' in the conundrum of melancholy and beauty in chapter 1, become a pernicious elevation of suffering to aesthetic pleasure.

Religious Melancholy

Just like love melancholy, religious melancholy often involves unrequited love – in this case, a love for god. There is a desire for a connection with god, but also a knowledge of the impossibility of such closeness. Relationship problems with deities extend back to classical times, when the Olympian gods were near, yet elusive. Identifying the figure of Apollo in a de Chirico painting (*The Enigma of the Oracle,* 1910), Toohey and Toohey ascribe to him a metonymic quality, that he stands for all gods, and shows their sometimes aloof relationship with humanity. The gods know 'how to cure our nostalgia and melancholy and how to "get us home". But they will not provide us with the answer.'[25] The relationship between this figure of Apollo, and the poignant figure of Odysseus nearby in the painting, engulfed in his nostalgia, sets up a *mise-en-scène*[26] that epitomises the predicament of humanity alienated from deities.

The parallel with love melancholy was captured by the tenth-century Arab physician Isaac (Ishaq ibn Imran), who also described a variety of religious melancholy, observing that, 'There are many holy and pious men who become melancholy owing to their great piety and from fear of God's anger or owing to their great longing for God until this longing masters and overpowers the soul; their whole feeling and thoughts are only of God, the contemplation of God, His greatness and the example of His perfection. They fall into melancholy as do lovers and voluptuaries, whereby the abilities of both soul and body are harmed, since the one depends on the other.'[27]

One of the most profound moments of religious melancholy was the experience of Spanish mystic, St John of the Cross. *Dark Night of the Soul* was written while he was incarcerated in a small cell, and embodies the yearning, through spiritual attainment, for a union with God. St John of the Cross described two dimensions of melancholy, one which was experienced on the path to spiritual fulfilment, and the other which led to deeper despair and resignation. It was this first type which is the 'spiritual melancholy' that came of the need for mystics to passively submit to God, and through this submission to experience a period of melancholy detachment from any joy in religion or in the world God has created. He also experienced the second kind of melancholy, which has been retrospectively diagnosed as depression, and he was adamant that this melancholy of despair was not caused by demons, and that it required a medical rather than spiritual intervention.

The melancholy that comes from the difficulties of relating to god persisted, and was interpreted as either a punishment or a test that had to be endured. Religious melancholy often brought extreme despair, as in the case in eighteenth-century New England where a woman was so beside herself about the problems of her relationship with God that she hung herself with a fishing line.[28]

The scenario for religious melancholy can also be seen to be the predicament of '*deus absconditus,*' or 'missing god' – literally the belief that god has absconded, and that we are abandoned. The absence of god leads to feelings of eternal and unresolvable loss, and a yearning to make contact. In some religions this sense of an unattainable love for god becomes expressed as a form of divine ecstasy. This melancholic yearning is sometimes shown in devotional works, as love poetry written to the Divine, of imagined moments of engagement and separation with this absent god. There is also the understanding that melancholy is associated with the introspection required for deep religious engagement, including receiving divine grace and in some cases mysticism and prophecy. A further aspect is that of frustration, of not being able to sufficiently honour or be close to god. In the Sufi religion, for example, a true Sufi follower is suffused with *hüzün*[29] because 'he suffers from grief, emptiness and inadequacy because he can never be close enough to Allah, because his apprehension of Allah is not deep enough'.[30]

Tristitia

In Latin, *tristitia* means sorrow, or to make sad, and its links to melancholy are immediately obvious. However, *tristitia's* unique sense of sadness and sorrow has all but disappeared over the centuries, often being folded into the general umbrella of melancholy. As noted above, *acedia* and *tristitia* were synonymous for many centuries, until *tristitia* assumed the sense of noble suffering, or what John

Cassian called 'wholesome sorrow'.[31] So while *acedia* was known as the sin of Sloth, *tristitia* was the sin of Sadness. It was considered a sin because it leads to despair, and inexorably to death, and the waste of life.

There is also a constructive interpretation to the idea of *tristitia*, as in the writings of Thomas More on Christ's own life of sadness. More's book *De Tristitia Christi* celebrates 'Christ's exemplary display of sadness, weariness and fear (*tristitia tedio puarore*) leading up to and during his crucifixion'.[32] More argued that our life should be one of sadness and not happiness, as we should not seek heaven on earth.

While both *acedia* and *tristitia* were best known during medieval times, and are words little used today, they are both underpinnings of one of melancholy's allies, *ennui*. This particular term is explored as part of the next chapter, in which the specific cultural colourings of melancholy are investigated, and how these in turn have had broader cultural influence.

Ubi sunt

Meaning literally 'where are?', *ubi sunt* is a lament over the imminent loss of things. The Latin phrase was used in medieval poetry to signal this type of sadness with its plaintive tone, and would usually be followed by a litany of lost things. It is shorthand for a longer phrase, *Ubi sunt qui ante nos fuerunt?* – 'Where are those who were before us?' The elegiac phrase is sung in the academic anthem *Gaudeamus Igitur,* the second verse of which begins, *Ubi sunt qui ante nos / In mundo fuere?* or 'Where are they / Who were in the world before us?'

The *ubi sunt* motif persists as a form which announces

a lamentation, or a sometimes nostalgic reverie. For example, from Laurence Sterne's *Tristram Shandy*: "'Where is Troy and Mycenae and Thebes and Delos and Persepolis and Agrigentum," continued my father, taking up his book of post-roads, which he had laid down. "What is become, brother Toby, of Nineveh and Babylon, of Cizicum and Mitylenae?"' And again in Shakespeare's *Macbeth*: 'The Thane of Fife had a wife: where is she now?' And in John Keats' *Autumn*, 'Where are the songs of Spring? Ay where are they?'[33]

   Peter Schwenger identifies a contemporary *ubi sunt* in George Perec's *Life: A User's Manual* where the character Serge Valène, a painter, recalls a lengthy list of things which have passed through his 55 years of residence in the apartment building: 'Where were they now, the Van Houten cocoa tins, the Banania cartons with the laughing infantryman, the turned-wood boxes of Madeleine biscuits from Commercy? Where were they gone, the larders you used to have beneath the window ledge, the packets of Saponite…'[34]

Notes

1. Werner Herzog, *Where the Green Ants Dream*.
2. Cited in Anton J van Hoff, *From Autothanasia to Suicide: Self-Killing in Classical Antiquity*, p.122.
3. Antonio Contreras Mas, *Libro de la Melancholía* by Andrés Velázquez (1585). Part 1. The intellectual origins of the book, p.31.
4. Psalm 91:6 in the St James version of *The Bible*. In some writings the 'noonday' reference is ascribed to Psalm 90:6, which depends on the particular translation.
5. Giorgio Agamben, *Stanzas: Word and Phantasm in Western Culture*, p.3.
6. Stanley W Jackson, *Melancholia and Depression: From Hippocratic Times*

to *Modern Times*, p.72.

7. John de Graaf, David Wann & Thomas H. Naylor, *Affluenza: The All-Consuming Epidemic.*

8. Interview with Georges Minois by Blandine Bénard, Chantal Tchoungi and Jacques Balducci, translated by Aris Sarafianos, in 'The Many Colours of Black Bile: the melancholies of knowing and feeling', p.1.

9. Clive Hamilton and Richard Denniss, *Affluenza: when too much is never enough.*

10. See Erwin Panofsky, *Meaning in the Visual Arts*. And see also Louis Marin, *Sublime Poussin.*

11. Anthony Blunt, 'Reviewed work(s): Poussin's *Et in Arcadia Ego*', p.96.

12. Bernard H Smith, *European Vision and the South Pacific*, p.45.

13. Virgil, *Virgil: Eclogues. Georgics. Aeneid 1-6*, p.273.

14. Avicenna in Stanley Jackson, *Melancholia and Depression: From Hippocratic Times to Modern Times*, p.355.

15. Johann Wolfgang von Goethe, *The Sorrows of Young Werther*, p.93.

16. Stendhal, *Love*, p.225.

17. In John Livingston Lowes, 'The Loveres Maladye of Hereos', p.492.

18. ibid, p.546.

19. Janelle L Wilson, *Nostalgia: Sanctuary of Meaning*, p.21.

20. Svetlana Boym, *The Future of Nostalgia*, p.13.

21. Frances Yates, *The Art of Memory*, p.59.

22. ibid, page 69.

23. Imannuel Kant in Edward Casey, *Remembering: A Phenomenological Study*, p.201.

24. Rainer Maria Rilke in Gaston Bachelard, *The Poetics of Space*, p.57.

25. Peter Toohey and Kathleen Toohey, 'Giorgio de Chirico, Time, Odysseus, Melancholy, and Intestinal Disorder', p.288-289.

26. *Mise-en-scène* is a term from theatre, also applied to cinema, which means the composition of a particular scene, including all of the scenery, props, lighting, and the actors in costume.

27. In Stanley W. Jackson, *Melancholia and Depression*, p.59.

28. Mary Ann Jimenez, 'Madness in Early American History: Insanity in Massachusetts from 1700-1830'.

29. Hüzün is a Turkish form of melancholy, discussed in chapter 4.

30. Orhan Pamuk, *Istanbul: Memories of a City*, p.81.

31. In Jackson (1986), *Melancholia and Depression*, p.68.

32. Douglas Trevor, *The Poetics of Melancholy in Early Modern Europe*, p.57.

33. Sterne, Shakespeare and Keats examples from Frederick Tupper, 'Ubi sunt-A Belated Postscript', p.198.

34. Peter Schwenger, *The Tears of Things: Melancholy and Physical Objects*, p.108.

From *Apea* to *Weltschmerz*:
A Lexicon of Melancholy

Laurence Aberhart, *Interior, Otago Museum, Dunedin,*
4 May 1994

From *Apea* to *Weltschmerz*:
A Lexicon of Melancholy

*The four and twenty letters make no more variety of words in
diverse languages, than melancholy conceits produce diversity of
symptoms in several persons. They are irregular, obscure, various, so
infinite … you may as well make the moon a new coat, as a true
character of a melancholy man…*
Robert Burton, *The Anatomy of Melancholy*[1]

Elusively sliding through time and space, melancholy
takes on many guises and colourings throughout history
and in different cultures. Melancholy evades precise definition, instead gathering up layers and layers of accretions.
As with any emotion, the question of universal experience is a perplexing one. What might it mean if an emotion, a condition, is not directly translatable from one
language to another? Is that same emotion experienced
differently by another language group, or perhaps
not even experienced at all? How much are language and
character associated? And what of those pheno-
mena which transcend language – painting and music for
example – might the emotions expressed in such works
take on a collectively felt response, an emotional
Esperanto?

Such questions are dissected within the fields of cross-
cultural psychology and linguistics, and hang like a threatening cloud over every literary translation, where the

particular poetic nuances of a work in one language must somehow be wrought into a different vocabulary and syntax. There are some emotions which are considered 'basic' – happiness and sadness, for example – and some cross-cultural linguists argue that some concepts are culture-specific and others are universal. Feeling, wanting and knowing are classified as universal concepts, whereas the Russian word *toska* – a type of melancholy – is culture-specific.[2]   It is beyond the scope of this book to dissect these arguments, and the intention is instead to present the richness of melancholy as it slips and slides through a range of languages.

The following lexicon traverses a range of different cultural expressions in order to construct a sense of the emotional ambience of melancholy and its attendant spirits. Many of the words in the lexicon presented here will be familiar to English speakers, as they have entered the English vocabulary as carriers of specific connotations of melancholy.   Melancholy, in its vague precision, has remained a relatively constant constellation of ideas throughout history. As Jennifer Radden notes, the discourse on melancholy has crossed between a breadth of cultures, Eastern and Western, and there have been multitudes of dialogues, from ancient to modern languages, yet, throughout all of this the ideas do not vary widely.[3] And during the two-thousand-year development of the term, as Klibansky, Panofsky and Saxl explain, 'Although new meanings emerged, old meanings did not give way to them; in short, it as a case not of decay and metamorphosis, but of parallel survival.'[4] This is not to say that there are not contradictions, and indeed contradiction is embedded within the concept of melancholy, but these have remained as constant points of tension.

Chinese

Autumn is the season most often associated with melancholy, invoking the sense of things passing, of imminent decline. In Chinese, there is a particular melancholic sadness tied to autumnness, in the concept of *bei qiu*, where *bei* is sadness and *qiu* is autumn. Autumn's potency for melancholy relates to the way in which life is paralleled to the seasons, a concept which is particularly strong in Chinese culture. The tradition of *bei qiu* was developed in the second century BC, by Song Yu, for example in the fragment, *Bei zai qui shi qi ye! Xiaose xi, cao mu yao luo er bian shuai!*, translated as:

> Alas for the breath of autumn!
> Wane and drear!
> Flower and leaf fluttering fall and turn to decay[5]

Ai is a further colouring of sadness in Chinese, one more closely aligned with ideas of grief and mourning, and particularly associated with a tangible sense of death. Keeping in mind Freud's distinction between mourning and melancholy, *ai* is more like a simple form of grief, where a sense of closure is reached. However, a third sense of sadness, *chou*, evokes that less tangible grief that is the mark of melancholy. This wound-kept-open version of sadness appears in a poem by Li Bai, the 'immortal poet' of the eighth century: *Chou dao dua shui shui gengliu, ju bei jiao chou chou geng chou. Rensheng zai shi bu cheng yi, ming shqo san fa nong bian zhou,* where the repetition of *chou* is expressed as layers of sadness and loneliness, of being inconsolable, melancholic:

> I lift my goblet to melt away sorrow,
> but sorrow continues in sorrow.
> Man's life in this world may never find
> what satisfies the mind –
> Tomorrow at dawn let your hair flow down,
> For delight sail off in your tiny boat.[6]

Chou takes on a range of melancholic colourings, including homesickness and nostalgia, or *xiang chou* – 'hometown *chou*'. Tied up with the sense of blackness and bleakness, *chou* is expressed as endless, like the seemingly interminable darkness of night. *Chou*'s interminability is precisely melancholy: 'Unlike *bei*, which is easy for the experiencer to get over, *chou* stays with the experiencer.'[7] One of the most evocative poets on the melancholy of *chou* is the eleventh/twelfth century poetess, Li Qingzhao. *Chou* appears throughout her poems, including the woeful lament '*Sheng Sheng Man*', or 'Every Sound Lentamente'. Using a metaphorical evocation of the bleakness of dismal weather and the passage of chrysanthemum flowers that even 'three cups of thin wine' could not alleviate, she finishes, *Zhe cidi, zen y ge chou zi liaode!*, translated as, 'How in the word "miserable", can one find / The total effects of all these on the mind.'[8] And like the emblematic head-in-hands posture of the melancholic, as described in Chapter 2 *chou* has its own physical expression, *chou mei*, or 'chou eyebrows', a visage of intense contemplation of an unsolvable and confusing problem.

English

The English word 'melancholy' is a legacy of the Greek terms *melas* (black) and *chole* (bile). Yellow bile, black bile, phlegm and blood constituted the four 'humours', and an imbalance in any of these constituted a disorder, with an excess of black bile being the condition of melancholy. Intriguingly, black bile appears to be an invented substance, a theoretical locus for the pathology of pathos, while all the other humours are identifiable within the body.

Variations of the word can be found in a variety of languages as a transliteration of the original Greek, such that in addition to the unique language-specific words outlined elsewhere in this lexicon there are also generic versions of the word 'melancholy': the French have *mélancolie,* the Italians *malinconia*, Germans *melancholie,* and so on. Despite the seemingly transparent etymology, the word has gathered around it a whole swarm of connotations, including the negative associations of depression. As alluded to in the introduction, this is a grey area, and presents a set of questions which are different to those explored by this book. Yet, such debates serve to illustrate the ongoing intangibility of 'melancholy', reinforced further by the various cultural colourings outlined in this lexicon. Central to all of this is the idea of sadness without purpose, without any apparent occasion, or at least out of proportion to its cause. The irresolvability of the cause is vital – as otherwise melancholy simply slips away into mourning and thus, eventually, closure.

Melancholy's specifically English connection is rooted in the legacy of Timothy Bright, Robert Burton, and the

Shakespearean evocation of the melancholy individual. One term that captures this tradition comes from the work of George Cheyne, an early researcher on psychiatry. The title of his 1733 book underscored what was considered a particular cultural association with melancholy: it was called *The English Malady*. His focus was on nervous debility, and through identifying it as a characteristic of the elite classes, is often seen as glamorising 'melancholy *à la mode*'.[9] Cheyne's 'English Malady' was a very social melancholy, a popularisation of the earlier visions of the melancholy genius, and Samuel Johnson was sceptical of such a construction, warning James Boswell, 'Do not let him teach you the foolish notion that melancholy is a proof of astuteness.'[10]

'Spleen' is a dimension of melancholy which was later adopted by the French, and is based on a physiological connection, since it is the spleen which, in the arcane language of Burton, 'draws this black choler [melancholy] to it by a secret virtue, and feeds upon it, conveying the rest to the bottom of the stomach, to stir up appetite, or else to the guts as an excrement'.[11] Spleen was a constituent of Cheyne's 'English Malady,' and poets like Matthew Green, known as 'Spleen Green', wrote about the prevention of spleen in 1737: 'how to drive away/The day-mare Spleen, by whose false pleas/Men prove mere suicides in ease/ And how I do myself demean/In stormy world to live serene.'[12]

The idea of spleen as a synonym for melancholy appears in English poetry of the eighteenth and early nineteenth centuries, but later begins to fade. One of the purest statements is in Wordsworth's autobiographical poem, *The Prelude,* begun in 1805, with its:

Moods melancholy, fits of spleen, that loved
A pensive sky, sad days, and piping winds,
The twilight more than dawn, autumn than spring;
A treasure and luxurious gloom of choice[13]

Finnish

The Finns have two words which carry melancholic
meaning – *apea* and *kaiho*. *Apea* is a feeling of sadness, of
being downcast and gloomy, while *kaiho* suggests a less
tangible poignancy, of yearning, longing, pining. The
emotion of *kaiho* is the central theme of the Finnish tango,
embracing solitude and loneliness. The Finnish tango is a
national phenomenon, the music of choice for over half
of Finland's population of 5 million. Writing in *Billboard*
magazine, Antti Isokangas described how a fusion of cultural influences is found in the Finnish tango, with the
conservative, stubborn and serious traits of Nordic peoples
complemented by 'Eastern European melancholy, pessimism, and even a strange, Arctic kind of masochism…'[14]
A 1993 *60 Minutes* programme profiled the Finnish tango,
reporting that dancing the tango in Finland was an
expression of 'clinical shyness [and] almost terminal
melancholy'.[15] Played mainly in minor keys, that musical
mode which is suffused with melancholy, the lyrics reinforce the sense of pathos which makes the Finnish tango
culturally distinct from the Argentinean tango. For the
Finns, the tango is about the love of longing, nostalgia,
unrequited love, and self-pity.

The Finnish architect Vesa Honkonen worked with
American architect Steven Holl on Helsinki's Kiasma
museum in the 1990s. One of Honkonen's tasks was to

convey the Finnish character to Holl, which he did via a letter, explaining in particular the pessimistic darkness of the Finnish people, and how the tango captures this:

> Ladies sitting at the other side of the outdoor dancing place Tanssilava. Men at the other side. No one smiles. Tango starts; men make their choices. No one speaks, just a nervous bow, girl moves her head a few millimetres meaning yes, and the dance starts... The world around does not exist anymore; the lyrics take one to the world of truth, the world of beautiful sorrow.[16]

French

The French concept of *ennui* is one which has assimilated itself into the English language, often translated as 'boredom'. Boredom and melancholy are closely associated, yet melancholy lacks the nihilism of boredom – or, as Svensden puts it, 'Boredom lacks the charm of melancholy' – a charm that is connected to melancholy's traditional link to wisdom, sensitivity and beauty.[17] *Ennui* could be considered 'lite' melancholy, lacking the gravity of a melancholy borne of self-inspection or critical reflection. Instead, *ennui* tends to be associated with a self-absorbed dissatisfaction with things. Often connected to the condition of modernity, *ennui*, like the Italian *noia,* has connotations of the effect of anaesthesia, the numbing boredom with the *taedium vitae* or weariness with the 'tediousness of life', and of *anhedonia* – an inability to find pleasure in things that should be pleasurable.

Tristesse is another French inflection of melancholy. This sense of sadness was personified in the figure of

Tristesse, one of the painted images encountered in the walled garden in the thirteenth-century poem, the *Roman de la Rose*. Amongst this group, all representing the defects which prevent courtly love and including 'Envy' and 'Avarice', *Tristesse* or 'Sorrow' is 'pale and gaunt... she did not want to be consoled at any price nor let go of the sorrow she had in her heart; she had angered her heart too much, and her grief was too deep rooted.'[18]

Michel de Montaigne, the sixteenth-century French essayist, used the term in his *Sur la tristesse*, translated as 'On Sadness' or 'Of Sorrow'. He saw *tristesse* as a fashionable affectation, an attempt at feigning the melancholy of genius. Montaigne distinguished melancholy from *tristesse*, noting that he suffers from the former, but not the latter. *Tristesse* is seen as the cause of violent passions, and Montaigne recounts a number of stories illustrating how it leads people to behave inappropriately.[19]

Françoise Sagan's first novel *Bonjour Tristesse*, published in the 1950s, captured the suspended quality of sadness in the title itself, and underscores the connection to melancholy in the first lines:

A strange melancholy pervades me to which I hesitate to give the grave and beautiful name of sadness. In the past the idea of sadness has always appealed to me, now I am almost ashamed of its complete egoism. I had known boredom, regret, and at times remorse, but never sadness. Today, it envelops me like a silken web, enervating and soft, which isolates me.[20]

For French anthropologist Claude Lévi-Strauss, *tristesse* was a quality found in entire cities, a collective melancholia.

In *Tristes Tropiques*, Lévi-Strauss conveys his feelings of futility in encountering the settlements beyond the margins of Western civilisation, speaking of his *tristesse*. This was not simply sadness, but a complex of lingering contemplation, and grief. Wandering through the world of these untouched cultures, Lévi-Strauss wrote that he returned with a handful of ashes, that all around him he saw the marks of monocultures, of 'civilisation produced in bulk'. The translators of *Tristes Tropiques* have always left the title in French, as requested by the author himself. One translation of the work, by John and Doreen Weightman, notes that, 'The possible English versions, such as "Sad Tropics", "the Sadness of the Tropics", "Tragic Tropics", etc., do not quite correspond either in meaning or in implication... the suggestion of "Alas for the Tropics!"'[21]

Although it is an English word, the emphasis on 'spleen' is a particularly French contribution to the lexicon of melancholy. French poet Charles Baudelaire used the word 'spleen,' in English, in his poetry to evoke the black pit of melancholy. Several poems in his collection *Les Fleurs du Mal* are titled *Spleen*, and call to mind the language of melancholy: 'When the low, heavy sky weighs like a lid', 'Hope like a bat / Goes beating the walls with her timid wings / And knocking her head against the rotten ceiling, and Hope, vanquished, / Weeps', and 'atrocious, despotic Anguish / On my bowed skull plants her black flag'.[22]

Baudelaire's collection of prose poems, published posthumously, was titled *Le Spleen de Paris,* and gathered together the sensations and responses to trying to find beauty in the modern city. His apparent guilt at witnessing poverty and deprivation serves to conjure up feelings of melancholy both in himself, and in the city by analogy, in a similar way to Claude Lévi-Strauss's sensing of *'tristesse'* in tropical cities. In witnessing an old clown on the streets of Paris he described how he saw him 'bent, decrepit, the ruin of a man, leaning against one of the posts of his cabin; a cabin more miserable than that of the lowest savage, and in which two candle ends, guttering and smoking, lighted only too well its penury.'[23] This sight affected Baudelaire with its intense melancholy, its spleen, and he grappled with his feelings of pity and sudden depression.

Spleen's resonance with the physiology of bile is echoed in EM Cioran's notion of *amertume* or 'gall', which offers a further French inflection of melancholy. Cioran originated from Romania, but spent much of his writing life in Paris, writing in French. His book of aphorisms, *Syllogismes d'Amertume* is translated by Richard Howard as *All Gall is Divided*, drawing the connection between the spleen and gall, both sites of the production and storage of bile, and their connections to melancholy and bitterness. And like Baudelaire's *Spleen de Paris,* Cioran's *Syllogismes d'Amertume* is a series of short, intense, meditations on melancholy and the allied themes of love, death, religion.

German

The melancholy sense of detachment from the world, the angst of disempowerment, is embodied in the German *Weltschmerz*. This agony of existence (*Welt* = world, *schmerz* = pain) is a pessimistic perspective on the evils of the world. The compound word was constructed by German novelist Jean Paul, in his novel *Titan* (1800-1803), to describe the unrequited love of the character Roquairol. This initial version of *Weltschmerz* was limited to this personal horizon, but its diffusion across Europe saw its melancholic meaning expand to the more generally pervasive existential gloom. Braun describes it in his treatise on the topic as 'the poetic expression of an abnormal sensitiveness of the feelings to the moral and physical evils and misery of existence – a condition which may or may not be based upon a reasoned conviction that the sum of human misery is greater than the sum of human happiness. It is usually characterised also by a certain lack of will-energy, a sort of sentimental yielding to these painful emotions.'[24]

The term for longing in German is *Sehnsucht*, combining a typically paradoxical melancholy mix of nostalgia and desire. CS Lewis adopted the word to express a form of spiritual longing throughout his life, from the works of Plato to a longing for God. The conundrum of *Sehnsucht* is further confounded as Lewis uses it synonymously with joy.

Wehmut and *Schwermut* are also used to convey melancholy, with the former being a lighter form and the latter darker, more aligned with the sense of depression. *Schwermut* has a specific weight to it, with part of the word, *Schwer*, meaning 'heavy'. German aesthetic theorist Theodor Adorno used *Schwermut* rather than *Melancholie* to refer to melancholic Dane, Søren Kierkegaard, in order to express the utter despair in his writings.

Japanese

The Japanese language has numerous words associated with melancholy. Expressing the subtle nuances within the complexity of melancholy, the words range through subjective qualities of the self, to the melancholy which is embedded in objects. Hagiwara Sakutorō, a poet from the early twentieth century, infused his poetry with many senses of melancholy. He used *kanashii* in the feeling of the sadness of things, as in his poem *Kanashii enkei*, 'Sad Vista', which describes 'the crowds of factory workers who spill out onto the pavements of the city at sunset, their hats casting shadows which spread out to encompass the whole city in a single dark pall'.[25] The title of his anthology *Aoneko* (1923) is translated as 'Blue Cat' and, in a late edition of the book, Sakutorō wrote about how that 'blue' was very much associated with the sense of melancholy. He also explained that, during this time of writing, he was deeply affected by Schopenhauer, and *Aoneko* is 'infused with a natural undercurrent of world weariness, the pessimistic, idle *ennui* which is the essence of his philosophy of denial of the will, or like the Hinayana Buddhist tenet of enlightenment through annihilation'.[26] In the *Aoneko*, or 'Blue Cat', anthology the word *yūutsu* is often used, to mean melancholy, as opposed to *kodoku* meaning solitude, loneliness or isolation, as used in his earlier anthology, *Tsuku ni hoeru* 'Howling at the Moon' (1917).

The melancholy of nostalgia is approximated in *natsukashii*, a word which doesn't have a direct parallel in English, but circles around sentimentality, longing for the past, and the recollection of good memories. *Natsukashii* is made up of 'vivid memories, the smell and taste of brief moments in the past such as are invoked by Marcel Proust's description of savoring a little oval 'Madeleine' Madeira cake...'[27]

The melancholy that is within objects and places, what might be considered the 'tears of things', is captured in the Japanese *wabi sabi*, which amplifies the significance of time passing and the pathos that this evokes. Andrew Juniper describes how *wabi sabi* 'is an expression of the beauty that lies in the brief transition between the coming and going of life, both the joy and melancholy that make up our life as humans.'[28] Inherent in this melancholic time-centredness is the inexplicable beauty of the weathered and the withered, a faded flower, the patina on a stone, a well-worn kitchen bowl.

The pathos that is implanted in things is also expressed in *mono no aware*, closely related to *wabi sabi*, and a Japanese version of *lacrimae rerum*. One of the core themes of *mono no aware* is serenity in the face of impermanence. Rather than the recognition that time passing and things disappearing bring an existential anguish, it is embodied as an aesthetic pleasure. The significance of Japanese rituals – the cherry blossom festival and the tea ceremony – lies within the melancholy of *mono no aware,* of the engaging with the poignant impressions made by fleeting, momentary experiences. Two key literary works express the idea of *mono no aware:* the eleventh century *The Tale of Genji*, sometimes called the world's first novel, and *The Tale of Heiki*, written by Kakuichi, a blind monk, in 1731. The lamentation of *mono no aware* is captured in the opening lines of *The Tale of Heiki*:

The sound of the Gion Shōja bells echoes the impermanence of all things; the color of the *śāla* flowers reveals the truth that the prosperous must decline. The proud do not endure, they are like a dream on a spring night; the mighty fall at last; they are as dust before the wind.[29]

Portuguese

Saudade is a vague, nostalgic melancholy. It is yet another term which is elusive and slippery, resonating strongly with melancholy. In the Portuguese dictionary written by lexicographer Antonio Houaiss, *saudade* is defined as 'melancólico de incompletude'[30] or a 'melancholy of incompleteness'. The definition extends this to a situation of deprivation, as in the loss of someone or something, or the lack of certain experiences. Such an absence can become 'the most profound presence in one's life', and it is a 'state of being, rather than merely a sentiment'.[31]

Fifteenth-century chronicler Duarte Nunes de Leão said that, '*Saudade* is the memory of something or the desire for something', as opposed to the less expansive definition of it by the romantic poet Almeida Garret as 'bitter pleasure' or 'pain and happiness'.[32] *Saudade* was the central theme of the Portuguese literary movement called *saudosimo* which was led by poet Teixeira de Pascoaes, and included the writer Fernando Pessoa. Because of *saudade's* particularly Portuguese flavour, the *saudosimo* movement saw it as central to the development of a local style of writing, and it became emblematic of the renaissance of Portuguese culture. Pascoaes called it 'the very spiritual blood of the race'.[33] The spirit of *saudade* infuses Pessoa's poetry, exemplified in the lines, 'I love everything that was / Everything that no longer is…', and, in another poem,

'It's neither happiness nor pain this pain that makes me happy.'[34]

This complex of longing and sadness is expressed in the Portuguese tradition of the *fado*, the song of fate. One dimension of the *fado* is the intensification of the nostalgia of being away from home, sung by sailors or peasants on their long journeys, to 'express their *saudades* and their longing to return'.[35] Pinto de Carvalho describes how in the *fado*:

> Both words and music reflect the abrupt turns of fickle Fortune, the evil destiny of the unfortunate, the irony of fate, the piercing pangs of love, the poignancy of absence or despair, the profound sobs of discouragement, the sorrows of *saudade*, the caprices of the heart, and those ineffable moments when the souls of lovers descend to their lips and, before flying back on high, hover for an instant in a sweet embrace.[36]

Nick Cave finds *saudade* in the modern love song: 'We all experience within us what the Portuguese call *saudade*, which translates as an inexplicable longing, an unnamed and enigmatic yearning of the soul and it is this feeling that lives in the realms of imagination and inspiration and is the breeding ground for the sad song, for the love song.'[37]

Russian

The emotional timbre of Russian melancholic yearning is embodied in *toska,* an untranslatable emotion, with resonances with the Portuguese *saudade*. Ideas of language, culture and identity are intertwined, with the various melancholic inflections reflecting the contexts of cultural history and topography. For *toska,* this means an echo of the vast Russian geography, as well as an encapsulation of *duša,* the Russian soul.

Toska combines three dimensions – fear, melancholy/nostalgia, and boredom/revulsion. These three elements can be present in different amounts to make up the whole, such that *toska* in itself is an intricate and constantly metamorphosing emotional complex. The relationship of *toska* to other similar terms in the Russian language also lends further colourings to the place of melancholy within the psyche. It has a connection with *tošno,* which relates the feeling of melancholy as a metaphysical sickness – an unease of the soul – to a feeling of physical sickness.

In the Romantic era of Russian literature, *toska* is a central theme, encapsulating the desire for yearning. It suffuses the pages of Pushkin's *Eugene Onegin* and, in his translation of this novel-in-verse, Vladimir Nabokov describes *toska* in a note as 'a generic term for a feeling of physical or metaphysical dissatisfaction, a sense of longing, a dull anguish, a preying misery, a gnawing mental ache'.[38] Nabokov's explanation of *toska* traces the complex terrain of this emotion, contradictory, untranslatable:

No single word in English renders all the shades of *toska.* At its deepest and most painful it is a sensation of great spiritual anguish, often without any specific cause. At less morbid levels it is a dull ache of the soul, a longing for nothing to long for, a sick pining, a vague restlessness, mental throes, yearning. In particular cases it may be the desire for somebody or something specific, nostalgia, lovesickness. At the lowest level it grades into ennui, boredom … [39]

During Soviet times the danger of melancholic intro-spection became political, and *toska* was marginalised. It was permissible to express melancholic thoughts, but not if they implicated the political regime. Instead, politically correct emotions, collective happiness and gaiety for example, were to be expressed. The pressure to be happy brought about its own *toska,* and grief boiled under the surface. It was sometimes expressed in a 'ritual lament',[40] an autobiographical statement of the sorrows that are borne in life. Melancholy, though, is bound up with less-specific grief, rather than sadness-with-a-cause. And it is within *toska* that this amorphous mourning is located.

Another term used by Pushkin in *Eugene Onegin* is *skushno,* a soft, Muscovite pronunciation of *skuchno.* Nabokov glosses this as 'I'm dull' or 'I am ennuied', iden-tifying it as a sort of melancholic boredom.[41] In his story '*Skushno*', Gregor von Rezzori, a writer fluent in many languages including Russian and English, describes it as a word that is difficult to translate. He offers, 'it means more than dreary boredom: a spiritual void that sucks you in like a vague but intensely urgent longing.'[42] Von Rezzori limns *skushno* via an image of landscape, striving to cap-ture this elusive term:

In the sunshine-basking seasons, the landscape with its vast horizon was as beautiful as a park; under a wintry sky, aswarm with crows, it offered only melancholy leagues of farmland, plowed up into black clods; far away, beyond the snowy strips that marked the hollows in the rolling terrain, the black lines of woodlands stretched all the way to the mountains, twilight blue and barely visible at the milk-glass edge of the sky dome. It was just such a day, in late winter, that corresponded best to my mood of *skushno*.[43]

Boredom is also conveyed in the word *unynie*, another Russian term allied with melancholy. In his study of the writings of Gogol, Christopher Putney notes how *acedia*, the melancholy of boredom, is translated as *unynie*.[44] This word means 'despondency' and Anna Wierzbicka highlights how it lacks the yearning and longing of *toska*, and is more like the black hole of melancholy – depression.[45]

Spanish

The brooding and dark mood of Spanish music, its 'shadowy and palpitating' quality is located in the particular melancholy called *duende*. The elusiveness of melancholy is one of *duende's* significant characteristics, a quality that was defined not in Spanish, but by Johann Wolfgang von Goethe, in searching for words to describe Paganini's poignancy: 'A mysterious power which everyone senses and no philosopher explains.'[46] This definition became embedded within the idea of *duende* in the famous essay by Spanish poet, Federico García Lorca, *Play and Theory of the Duende*. Lorca connected *duende* directly with death: 'the *duende* does not come unless he sees that death is possible. The *duende* must know beforehand that he can serenade death's house and rock those branches we all wear, branches that do not have, will never have, any consolation.'[47]

Nick Cave finds the idea of the *duende* persists in

certain kinds of music, and is something that requires a particular attention: 'Sadness or *duende* needs space to breathe.' It is particularly connected to the melancholy of love, and, 'All love songs must contain *duende*. For the love song is never truly happy. It must first embrace the potential for pain.'[48]

Turkish

Orhan Pamuk's novel *Istanbul* is a remarkable, extended meditation on the city and, in particular, its melancholy or *hüzün*. As a form of collective melancholy, the 'black mood [felt] by millions of people together', *hüzün* engulfs the entire ancient city, imparting a particular colouring, mood, and zeitgeist. Pamuk enumerates the qualities of *hüzün* characterised in particular events or scenes in a sequence that runs to some 5½ pages, to include such moments as 'the evenings when the sun sets early'; 'the old Bosphorus ferries moored to deserted stations in the middle of winter, where sleepy sailors scrub the decks, a pail in their hands and one eye on the black-and-white television in the distance'; 'the clock towers no one ever notices'; and 'the fruits, vegetables, garbage and plastic bags and wastepaper, empty sacks, boxes and chests strewn across abandoned street markets on a winter evening'.[49] Pamuk also identifies the particular cultural ethos of *hüzün*, that, 'Istanbul does not carry its *hüzün*, as "an illness for which there is a cure" or an "unbidden pain from which we need to be delivered"; it carries its *hüzün* by choice, and with honour.'

Hüzün has a visual quality, it is 'black and white' – not in the sense of a frankness, but of a reduced tonal range evocative of the nostalgia that accompanies photography and film from the pre-colour era, that vision of the past having been monochromatic. This cultural suffusion of melancholy is very different from the idea of a personal psychic state – of depression as such. Pamuk describes how the setting of the city itself is *hüzün*, as though the city has a psychic state, and it comes through in the 'black-and-white' Bosphorus, and in the city's ruins.

Notes

1. Robert Burton, *The Anatomy of Melancholy*, p.247.
2. See for example Jean Harkins and Anna Wierzbicka (eds), *Emotions in crosslinguistic perspective*.
3. Jennifer Radden, *The Nature of Melancholy: From Aristotle to Kristeva*, p.ix.
4. Raymond Klibansky, Erwin Panofsky and Fritz Saxl, *Saturn and Melancholy: Studies in the History of Natural Philosophy, Religion and Art*, p.3.
5. Zhengdao Ye, 'An inquiry into sadness in Chinese', p.370.
6. Stephen Owens' translation cited in ibid, p.379.
7. ibid, p.384.
8. ibid, p.386.
9. Roy Porter, 'Introduction' in George Cheyne, *The English Malady*, p.xi.
10. In ibid.
11. Robert Burton, *An Anatomy of Melancholy*, p.25.
12. In Oswald Doughty, 'The English Malady of the Eighteenth Century', p.265.
13. ibid, p.267.
14. Antti Isokangas, 'Finnish Tango: Once a Fad, the Dance is now a Tradition', p.78.
15. Richard Wilkins, 'Cultural Frames: Loci of intercultural communication asynchrony in a CBS 60 Minutes news segment', p.243.

16. Vesa Honkonen, *A letter for Steven Holl to explain the behaviour of Finnish people.*

17. Lars Svensden, *A Philosophy of Boredom*, p.19.

18. Guillaume de Lorris and Jean de Meun, *The Romance of the Rose*, p.35.

19. See Michel de Montaigne, *The Complete Essays*.

20. Françoise Sagan, *Bonjour Tristesse*, p.3.

21. Translators' Note in Claude Lévi-Strauss, *Tristes Tropiques*, p.11.

22. Charles Baudelaire, *The Flowers of Evil*.

23. Charles Baudelaire, *Paris Spleen*, p.26.

24. Wilhelm Alfred Braun, *Types of Weltschmerz in German Poetry*, p.1.

25. Hagiwara Sakutorō in Hugh Clark (2003) 'Sakutorō and the City', p.144.

26. ibid, p.149.

27. Ingrid Fritsch, '*Chindonya* Today: Japanese Street Performers in Commercial Advertising', p.65.

28. Andrew Juniper, *Wabi-Sabi: The Japanese Art of Impermanence*, p.1.

29. Kakuichi, *The Tale of the Heiki*, p.23.

30. Antonio Houaiss, *Dicionario Houaiss da lingua portuguesa*.

31. Katherine Vaz, *Saudade*.

32. Darlene J Sadlier, *An Introduction to Fernando Pessoa: Modernism and the Paradoxes of Authorship*, p.139.

33. Maria Irene Ramalho, Sousa Santos, Irene Ramalho Santos, *Atlantic Poets: Fernando Pessoa's Turn in Anglo-American Modernism*, p.288.

34. ibid, p.139–140.

35. Ventura de Abrantes in Rodney Gallop, 'The Fado (The Portuguese Song of Fate)', p.203.

36. Pinto de Carvalho in ibid, p.200.

37. Nick Cave, *The Secret Life of the Love Song; The Flesh made Word*.

38. Aleksandr Sergeevich Pushkin, *Eugene Onegin*, Volume 2 of 4, p.337.

39. ibid, volume 1 of 4, p.141.

40. Golfo Alexopoulus cited in Shelia Fitzpatrick, 'Happiness and *Toska*: An Essay in the History of Emotions in Pre-war Soviet Russia', p.365.

41. Aleksandr Sergeevich Pushkin, *Eugene Onegin*, volume 2 of 4, p.63.

42. Gregor von Rezzori, *Memoirs of an anti-Semite*, p.1.

43. ibid, p.3.

44. Christopher R Putney, 'Acedia and the *Daemonium Meridianum* in Nikolaj Gogol's 'Povest' o tom, kak possorilsja Ivan Ivanovičs Ivanom Nikiforovičem', p.237.

45. Anna Wierzbicka, *Emotions Across Languages and Cultures: Diversity and Universals*, p.308, n.3.

46. Federico García Lorca, *In Search of Duende*, p.49.

47. Ibid, p.58.

48. Nick Cave, *The Secret Life of the Love Song; The Flesh made Word*.

49. Orhan Pamuk, *Istanbul: Memories of a City*, pp.84-89.

A 'Blue' Guide: Melancholy in
Cinema, Art, Literature, Music,
Architecture and Landscape

Laurence Aberhart, *Moreporks (Bird Skins Room #2),*
Taranaki St, Wellington, 3 October 1995

5

A 'Blue' Guide: Melancholy in Cinema, Art, Literature, Music, Architecture and Landscape

Melancholy hates haste and floats in silence. It must be handled with care. Nick Cave, *The Love Song*[1]

There is, art historian Jean Clair suggests, a whole theatre of melancholy, an ideal 'museum' of melancholy, and an ideal picture gallery of melancholy, which would include works 'from Albrecht Dürer to Edvard Munch, from Domenico Fetti to Giorgio de Chirico', and an imagined sculpture museum of melancholy which would display works from 'ancient steles with their grief-stricken mourners, hands tucked under arm-pits, down to Rodin's *Thinker*, sunk in his black thoughts'.[2] Clair's vision of an ideal picture and sculpture gallery was recently realised in his curation of the exhibition, *Mélancolie: Génie et Folie en Occident* ('Melancholy: Genius and Madness in the West'), staged at the Galeries Nationales du Grand Palais in Paris, and then in the Neue Nationalgalerie in Berlin, in late 2005 and 2006.

Beyond Jean Clair's observations, and further to the exhibition, there is also to be imagined perhaps, an ideal film festival of melancholy, a library of melancholy literature, a playlist of melancholy music, and a guidebook of architecture and landscapes which epitomise the qualities of melancholy. This final chapter of the *Field Guide* provides an overview of some of the manifestations of melancholy within the domain of creative expression. The works here constitute a desiderata of melancholy, a litany of the desired elements of such a state, a mood, a guide to the places of the blues.

The 'Blue Guide' cannot possibly provide an exhaustive list of all things melancholy, but seeks to point to things, particularly things which are outside the margins, and to illuminate them so that the various manifestations of the family resemblance might be recognised. The aspiration of the 'Blue Guide' is to open up a particular way of seeing and appreciating this vital aspect of the human condition, ways to experience the delicious elusiveness of melancholy.

A Film Festival of Melancholy

Reflecting on what might be included in a film festival of melancholy brings forth waves of different melancholic expressions. Within the medium of film, melancholy might be captured in the characters, the storyline, or the evocation of atmosphere and mood through the use of settings or particular tonality and sound. Batman, in his early incarnation, epitomises the archetypical melancholic character, as the dark and seemingly depressive hero, a modern-day Shakespearean tragic figure.

Films which use the impression of melancholy within the medium itself include the works of Bill Morrison and James Elaine. Morrison works with old film which has decayed, and in his short film *Light is Calling* (2004) a scene from the 1926 film *The Bells* is reprinted and set to a soundtrack by composer Michael Gordon. The disintegration of the old film becomes a thing of beauty and fascination, providing an abstract flux of blobs and forms, reminiscent of the surrealists' techniques of decalcomania and frottage. In the longer 2002 film, *Decasia*, its title a play on the words 'decay' and 'fantasia', Morrison used fragments of film found in the Fox Movietone Newsfilm Library in South California. The collaboration with composer Michael Gordon produced a haunting, pulsing, seething film, where the holes and flaws of the decomposing celluloid seemed almost like watching decay in action. The images writhe and flicker on the screen, with the various melting and fading surfaces overlaid over the top of sometimes barely recognisable scenes from the past. Images pulsate – whirling dervishes, a serene geisha, a boxer – and over it all the strange spectre of the bubbling emulsion, a cinematic ectoplasm which is in synchronicity with the haunting soundtrack. While there is no story to *Decasia*, there is the frame of the great melancholic narrative of modernity underscoring the sequence, with the headings as simple intertitles, 'Creation', 'Civilization', 'Conundrum' and 'Disintegration and Rebirth'.

James Elaine also uses old film but, in his case, he works with film stock that is itself from another era, rather than with exposed film footage in a state of decay. He used old Super 8 film to make the film *Melancholia* (2004) which was shot at the World's Fairgrounds in Flushing Meadows, Queens, New York. The soundtrack of the hauntingly repetitive piano composition by William Basinski, *The Saddest Melody Ever Heard*[3] is again critical to the melancholy effect of the film.

The reduction of technique is also a key to the melancholy ambience of the films *London* (1992) and *Robinson in Space* (1997) by Patrick Keiller. Both films are shot almost wholly without moving shots. Instead, they are composed of sequences of static camera shots – where the camera is set in one place and records the scene from that point, the lingering take sometimes devoid of human content. The movement of the River Thames, the customers in a shopping mall, London red buses, all filmed with an almost deadening slow pace. Nothing happens, in a conventional filmic sense. There is no denouement, no punch line. Only relentless tedium, the *ennui* of existence; melancholy alienation, loss, longing. The ghosts of previous visitors to the city are invoked – Baudelaire, Rimbaud – enhancing the melancholy atmosphere. In Keiller's films the decay is in the landscape itself, in the city fabric, the tragic spectacle of Thatcherite Britain, the IRA bombings, portrayed via various *mise-en-scènes*. The counterpoint to the film is not the melancholy music scores like those of Gordon or Basinksi, but the incredibly weighty voice of narrator Paul Scofield. Only one voice is heard during both films, and it is Scofield's: deep, gravelly, and inflected with the gravitas of melancholy, the tired voice of *Weltschmerz*. The pain of the world, of 1990s Britain, is conveyed in the slowly delivered words, the narration of a world gone awry.

The tedium of *Weltschmerz* also permeates the films of Italian director Michelangelo Antonioni. In films like *L'avventura* (*The Adventure*, 1960) and *Il deserto rosso* (*The Red Desert*, 1964) repetition and a sense of hollowness represent the characters' lives of *ennui* or *noia*. The characters' melancholy comes from the paradox of affluence, of an easy life with too much time on their hands, and Antonioni, the 'poet of *ennui*', mines the gap between contentment and nihilism. *The Red Desert* was set in the industrial zone of Ravenna, but Antonioni said he was not condemning the inhuman industrial world; instead he 'wanted to translate the poetry of that world, in which even factories can be beautiful … The neurosis I sought to describe in *Red Desert* is above all a matter of adjusting.'[4]

Swedish director Ingmar Bergman also explores the *ennui* of contemporary existence in the settings and characterisations of his films. In *From the Life of the Marionettes* (1980), the characters Peter and Katarina discuss the very nature of *ennui* itself. Katarina firstly says that she does not even know what *ennui* is, and Peter responds, 'I feel *ennui*, yes. And a typical component of *ennui* is that you feel an insurmountable *ennui* in explaining how *ennui* works.'[5] Beyond the melancholy of *ennui* there is a dark angst which characterises the Swedish culture, and permeates Bergman's films. A combination of a national character of detachment, against the strongly seasonal light, with the long white nights of summer and the enduring darkness of winter, evokes a particularly melancholy *genius loci*, a spirit of the place.

Bergman's films *Wild Strawberries* (1957) and *Shame* (1968) are pervaded with a sense of sorrow, of things passing, of the end of summer and the plunge into autumn, with the winter lying in wait beyond. In *Wild Strawberries*, the main character, Isak, is approaching death, and recalling his life, in day dreams, memories, a movement towards darkness. The final scene of *Shame* conveys a fatalistic relationship with the world, as the two characters, Jan and Eva, hold one another, recalling moments from the past. The final passage of Bergman's script reads: 'On the sev-

enth day a storm blows up, there is a heavy rain. The sur-
vivors slake their thirst with the poisoned water. [The
film ends].'[6] The bleak relationship with mortality is the
central theme of *Winter Light* (1963), with the priest,
Tomas, in a state of turmoil over his failing faith. His
counselling of one of his parishioners, Adam Persson,
ends catastrophically when Tomas's doubting is transferred
to the already morose Persson, whose nihilism stems from
reading about the Chinese having an atom bomb, and
about their growing sense of hatred. Tomas's bleak coun-
sel only adds to Persson's predicament, culminating in his
suicide. Tomas rails against 'God's silence', and expresses
the sense of religious melancholy, of a god who leaves him
lonely and abandoned.

Mortality, religion and death were explored to their
extremes in *The Seventh Seal* (1957). The contingency
of life was symbolically expressed in the chess game
which the knight, Antonius Block, played against Death,
literally playing for his life. Bergman's screenplay evokes
the sense of alienation and abandonment, a type of *deus
absconditus,* that is felt by the knight and colours the film:
'The knight returns to the beach and falls on his knees.
With his eyes closed and brow furrowed, he says his
morning prayers. His hands are clenched together and
his lips form the words silently. His face is sad and bitter.
He opens his eyes and stares directly into the morning
sun which wallows up from the misty sea like some
bloated, dying fish. The sky is gray and immobile, a dome
of lead. A cloud hangs mute and dark over the western
horizon. High up, barely visible, a seagull floats on
motionless wings.'[7]

The melancholy pervading the films of Russian direc-

tors Andrei Tarkovsky and Alexander Sukurov, and Greek
director Theo Angelopoulos, is a poetic, nostalgic imagery
from timeless places. Tarkovsky's haunting works are not
dependent on narrative for their melancholy, but on the
emotional content of the imagery. In his films *Nostalghia*
(1983) and *Mirror* (1975) the melancholy of memory suffuses the imagery, with fragments of houses, landscapes in
afternoon light, portrayed as misty recollections. Moments
of surrealistic reverie, rain, dripping water, the overturned
apple cart in *Ivan's Childhood* (1962), the strange water-
logged landscape of *Stalker* (1979). In *The Sacrifice* (1986),
Mirror and *Solaris* (1972), a figure levitates, defying our
connection with the physical present. Tarkovsky explained
the connections between his own nostalgia and that
which is present in *Nostalghia*, as 'a complex sentiment,
one that mixes the love for your homeland and the
melancholy that arises from being far away … I wanted
the film to be about the fatal attachment of Russians to
their national roots, their past, their culture, their native
places, their families and friends.'[8] Alexander Sokurov's
remarkable film *Russian Ark* (2002) was filmed in a single
take, moving through the halls and courtyards of St
Petersburg's Hermitage museum. As an historic narrative
it also embodies this melancholic connection between
Russians and their soil, the sense of *toska*.

Angelopoulos's first film *Reconstruction* (1970) explored
the relationship between Greeks and their landscape. The
film was based on a real village and conveyed the desolation occurring as part of the depopulation of the villages
in the Greek countryside during the mid-twentieth century. The themes of loss and displacement also appear in
his later film *The Weeping Meadow* (2004), a Greek tragedy,

as the refugees from Odessa make their way to New Odessa. As in the films of Tarkovsky, the images of rain and water-soaked landscapes evoke the intense nostalgia of the time. A floating funeral moves across a watery landscape, black flags tied to the boats, a massive flood engulfs the refugees' village. The buildings are left abandoned, derelict skeletons.

A Melancholy Art Exhibition

Melancholy in art is an enormous topic, with an overwhelming array of possible means to tackle it – chronologically, thematically, typologically, or even forensically. This latter approach could be deployed, metaphorically speaking, as an examination of images to discern their melancholic content. It could be possible to identify the evidence of melancholy in such a way, finding the clues within works. Dogs, bats and owls, for example, are bearers of melancholic content. The dog of Dürer's *Melencolia I* is a 'fellow sufferer', and the connection is made back to the dog hieroglyph of the Egyptian alphabet, which signified spleen. The dog is considered 'more gifted and sensitive than other beasts, has a very serious nature and can fall a victim to madness, and like deep thinkers is inclined to be always on the hunt, smelling things out, and sticking to them'.[9] Bats and owls appear at twilight, and are also connected with melancholy, and the frontispiece to Burton's *The Anatomy of Melancholy* includes a number of such creatures. On the other hand, a thematic exploration offers the opportunity to point out some family resemblances, and the 'Blue Guide' plots three particular dimensions of melancholy in art, one related to technique (low-tech), one to content (memory works), and one to subject matter (the empty and lonely).

Low-tech Photography

Photographs are inherently melancholy. They immediately evoke the past, things lost, memories, that which is 'dead' already, and Roland Barthes calls this 'the melancholy of Photography itself'.[10] Infused with the ache of absence, photographs are portals to fugitive moments, as in filmmaker Chris Marker's declaration, 'I claim, for the image, the humility and powers of a madeleine.'[11] Recalling Marcel Proust's iconic mnemonic moment in *Remembrance of Things Past*, where the small cake triggers childhood memories, Marker relates photography to the melancholy of memory, the unattainable presences of the past.

Old photographs in particular seem steeped in melancholy, their distance from the viewer more pronounced, perhaps faded, sepia-toned, other-worldly. The connection of melancholy and memory in photography represents the presence of 'aura', something that Walter Benjamin argued was lost when photographs moved from having value as part of the 'cult of remembrance' to succumbing to their 'exhibition value'. Aura inheres within the connectivity to intimacy, to the sense of an original, authentic presence, and Benjamin believes, 'It is no accident that the portrait was the focal point of early photography. The cult of remembrance of loved ones, absent or dead, offers a last refuge for the cult value of the picture. For the last time the aura emanates from the early photographs in the fleeting expression of a human face. This is what constitutes their melancholy, incomparable beauty.'[12]

The shift towards technology, and mass appreciation of art, transforms the quality of the image, and its distance from the receiver. With this goes the loss of its aura. There is a legacy of this loss in contemporary photography, a striving to reclaim that melancholic content, and this is often through a resistance to the available technology. As a contrast, the photographs aspire more to the rudimentary approach to photography which produces the kind of effects philosopher and art historian Hubert Damisch alludes to: 'It is no accident that the most *beautiful* photograph so far achieved is possibly the first image Nicéphore Niépce fixed in 1822, on the glass of the camera obscura – a fragile, threatened image, so close in organization, its granular texture, and its emergent aspect, to certain Seurats – an incomparable image which makes one dream of a photographic *substance* distinct from subject matter, and of an art in which light creates its own metaphor.'[13]

Niépce took his photograph with a 'camera obscura', literally a 'dark room', with an eight hour exposure. This pinhole camera technique is one of the means of bypassing technological precision, and used by photographers seeking an auratic content in their work. One particularly evocative set of images consists of those made by Volkmar Herre of Ian Hamilton Finlay's *Fleur de L'Air* project in Provence, France. The images Herre captured are achingly beautiful and evocative of a past golden age. Garden theorist John Dixon Hunt connects the process of taking the photographs in such a way, which requires a retardation of time, with the slowness that a garden represents – it is a place where time slides by slowly. He wrote, 'Simultaneously, and beyond the ineluctable quiddity or 'thingness'

of the rocks, trees and earth, the extraordinary light translates everything into praeternatural scenery.'[14]

American-based Japanese photographer Hiroshi Sugimoto also works against the grain of contemporary photography to capture an auratic quality. Through technical
adjustments of film speed, filters, and by using a wooden
cabinet camera, Sugimoto is able to reproduce the conditions of early nineteenth-century photography. In his
serenely beautiful seascape series, for example, Sugimoto
used exposures of an hour and a half to capture the image.
The photographs are otherworldly and, as suggested by
the title of his 2006 exhibition at the Mori Art Gallery in
Japan, the images evoke *The End of Time*. A further technique deployed by Sugimoto is to intentionally make the
photographs out of focus. Through making the focal point
twice the point of infinity, the images float within an
imprecise time and space. Just recognisable in the architecture series are the iconic forms of the Eiffel Tower, the
Guggenheim, the Empire State Building, Tadao Ando's
Church of Light, and Le Corbusier's Chapel of Notre
Dame du Haut.[15]

While Sugimoto returns to photography's origins to
create the conditions for melancholy's capture, even
recent technology is already gaining a nostalgic quality
that also allows for an eschewing of technical precision.
Invented in the late 1940s, Polaroid cameras became very
popular during the 1960s and 1970s, with the unique feature of instantly printing their own photographs. The
instantaneous feature of the Polaroid has now been
superseded by digital cameras, and the technology rapidly
moved into obsolescence, to the extent that in early 2008
Polaroid announced that the film for the cameras would

no longer be manufactured. The images taken with Polaroid cameras have an auratic quality in that each one is an original, rather than multiple prints from a negative, or prints that have been manipulated in a dark room, or more recently, digitally.

Filmmaker Andrei Tarkovsky created a body of photography using a Polaroid camera. The blurb for the book *Instant Light: Tarkovsky Polaroids* describes how the images capture moments from his life, for example those in Russia which 'have the radiant melancholy of lengthening shadows and trees looming through mystical dawns near [his] country dacha…'[16] The photographs in the book are remarkable transports of time and place, tracing the locations of film shoots, travels and domestic scenes. Screenwriter and companion of Tarkovsky, Tonino Guerra, wrote about one of the images which captures a moment in their travels through Italy, 'I remember when we entered the little church on the edge of the water-filled square, where the mist rising from the water gave a sense of distance to the landscape of ancient houses. The warm light that morning streamed through the dusty windows and came to rest on faded decorations on a wall. He surprised me sitting on a pew, as though I were just the right shadow to accentuate the caress of the sun beyond my dark body. These images leave with us a mysterious and poetic sensation, the melancholy of seeing things for the last time.'[17]

The disappearance of film for the Polaroid camera resonates with the work of British photographer Jacob Carter, who uses film stock which expired before 1970, utilising the unpredictable results as a means of bypassing technical precision. Disposable cameras are also very low-tech approaches to photography, allowing the exactness of digital imaging to be suppressed in favour of other presences. In a series called *Do You Realise* (2006) New Zealand photographer Patrick Reynolds used a disposable camera to capture images of his family's annual holiday to the seaside. It was the first time his father hadn't been able to come along on the holiday, due to his ill health, and the images were partly to show to him when they returned to the city. His father died soon after the photographs were released, suffusing these images of poignant nostalgia with an even deeper melancholy. The series title echoed the lyrics from a song by The Flaming Lips, and Reynolds said, '...I realised that the lyrics... summed up what I was feeling and therefore what I was trying to express with the photographs: beauty but with a shadow.'[18] Reynolds' images from the series are all black and white, vignetted, imperfect, and echo the qualities of his earlier monochromatic photographs in which '[v]ision is burdened with a corporeal melancholy'.[19]

Monochromatic photography can evoke a sense of time, nostalgia, a connection back to a pre-colour era, like Orhan Pamuk's description of Istanbul as 'black and white', as though the colour had drained out of the place itself. Laurence Aberhart uses black and white as a means of limning the world, so much so that one of his friends was surprised to look through his viewfinder one day and see the world was still in colour. Like the Bechers and Hiroshi Sugimoto, Aberhart uses an ancient, wooden, large format camera – a 100 year old 8 by 10 Korona view camera. In his images there is a sense of stillness, absence, pathos, 'deserted, empty. The people have gone, leaving only the cryptic remains of their culture. His New Zealand is a ghost town.'[20] Such a lingering contemplation of absence effects a powerful resistance to the culture of happiness, the carving of space for the shadowy, a withdrawal from the insistent cacophony of colour that intrudes on a meditative experience of the world. The images have the effect of obscuring rather than revealing, and they have aura. This is the antithesis of the actions of the 'contemporary masses', as Benjamin explained, of those who seek to 'pry an object from its shell, to destroy its aura', to remove the uniqueness from everything. Benjamin's definition of aura relates to a sense of distance, rather than a need to have everything close-up, revealed, exposed, as though 'while resting on a summer afternoon, you follow with your eyes a mountain range on the horizon or a branch which casts its shadow over you, you experience the aura of those mountains, that branch'.[21] And in Aberhart's photographs, the melancholy of aura is palpably there – in toning his photographs with gold in the early 1980s he achieved an effect 'like a light you sometimes encounter during the 'magic hour' of dusk, when lowering sun softens shadows, activates the light-sensitive edges of your visual field, and makes each leaf, stone and thing look uncannily present.'[22]

Memory works

Albums and archives also draw upon photography's melancholy evocation of times gone by, of the pathos of the dead-already. Barthes' vision of the photograph bringing back the dead, and Sontag's conception of the photograph as a 'death mask' infuse this particular medium with a profound mnemonic role. Even when the images encountered are not of familiar places or people, the photograph's memory task bestows upon it a melancholic dimension, such is the potent relationship between melancholy and memory.

The strange dislocation between viewing a photograph and not knowing the place or person pictured is echoed in the concept of 'found' photographs. Whether from newspapers, archives, or literally found on the street, 'found' photographs have a quality of anonymity, and their uniqueness further amplifies the aura of the original. When the 'found' photograph is used in a specific context, whether being exhibited in a gallery, or as an illustration in a book, it takes on the 'magic' of that setting in the way described by Marcel Duchamp in his development of the 'readymade'. German artist Gerhard Richter used an array of found photographs as the basis of his massive memory work, *Atlas* (1962-2006). Richter repainted the found photographs, in a photorealist manner, intensifying the effect of their anonymity. The photographs included 'found family snapshots and vacation photos, advertising and fashion photographs, news photos and celebrity shots by *paparazzi* (and even a photograph of the moon's surface from one of the Apollo missions).'[23] Richter organised his images onto panels within his *Atlas* project, sometimes illustrating a particular theme, such as landscapes or portraits. But other panels are more reminiscent of the arbitrary juxtapositions of objects in an archive, or images on a magazine page, or fragments of memory in the mind's eye.

Joseph Cornell juxtaposed texts, objects, photographs and ephemera, creating enigmatic mnemonic shadowboxes. The discarded objects of life are encapsulated within the boxes to create surreal *mise-en-scènes*, melancholy fragments of affective beauty. Mexican poet Octavio Paz wrote *Objects and Apparitions* for Cornell, describing these melancholic fragments:

Monuments to every moment,
refuse of every moment, used:
cages for infinity.

Marbles, buttons, thimbles, dice,
pins, stamps, and glass beads:
tales of the time.[24]

Like the tradition of *vanitas*[25] paintings, these items seem to bear the weight of a symbolic dimension, yet they are elusive and mysterious in their meaning. In *A Dressing Room for Gille* (1939), Cornell placed a cut-out of a reproduction, probably from a magazine, of Watteau's melancholy clown, Pierrot, or the Gilles. The Pierrot figure stands, looking awkward and poignant, against an array of harlequin-patterned papers, in this small room, this box of shadows. Another assemblage, *Object (Roses des Vents)* (1942-1953), appears at first like a collection of memorabilia from voyages to exotic places. This immediately brings a sense of melancholy, as some of the most intensely poignant moments of life come at the end of travels to other places. Yet, Cornell's box is even more melancholy, since these fragments are from journeys never taken. The lid of the box has a map of the Great Australian Bight, no doubt a place about as far away as Cornell could imagine from his home on Utopia Parkway in Queens, New York. The box itself is divided into a series of small compartments, covered by a panel which has twenty-one compasses, each with the needle pointing in a different direction. The compartments contain such curious things as an image of the moon, faraway peninsulas, enigmatic balls, and places marked with map pins. It is a memory work, a doleful diorama of an imagined exotic world.

Constructing memories from fragments, or infusing the works of the present with signs from the past, suspends them in time, gaining a sense of a frozen infinitude. The quality of aura bestows something arrestingly poignant upon them, and they can become melancholy emblems, touchstones. Anselm Kiefer's works draw in references, quotations, moments from the near and distant past. A group of sculptures, collectively titled *The Angel of History*, are vehicles for the past. On the wings of each of a group of fighter jets sculpted from lead are elements from the past: fragments of bygone eras, texts, teeth, hair, flowers and, most significantly, one of the jets carries an enigmatic polyhedron. It is the very same polyhedron that sits beside Albrecht Dürer's melancholy angel five centuries before, and the resonances echo: Kiefer's 1990-1 work is titled *Melancholia*.

It would be easy to fill an entire *Field Guide* with the melancholy qualities of Kiefer's work. There are layers upon layers of evocative referencing and formal manoeuvres which are suffused with the grey blackness of German melancholy – if not a German Autumn then perhaps a German Twilight. One of Kiefer's works is in fact titled *Abendland (Twilight of the West)*. The work is a built-up surface, a mixed media mélange of rubbing, paint and applied textures. Hovering above the horizon is a rubbing of a manhole cover from a past era, here standing in for the sinking sun. Twin rail tracks move up the page, merging then separating. And the whole sits within the alchemical moment of twilight, melancholy's time. The title is a reference to Oswald Spengler's book from 1918, *Der Untergang des Abendlandes,* translated as *The Downfall –* or *The Decline – of the West*. Spengler's sense of *Untergang* was in terms of a transitional time, a sunset (*sonnenuntergang*), or indeed, a twilight – the melancholy of things imminently lost. Kiefer's work therefore carries layers of melancholy baggage – while *Abendland* is technically the 'Occident', *Abend* is 'evening', which adds further weight to the image.

The memory of things, of cultures and places that have disappeared, of buildings and people, persists as a form of residue. Dowsers use a term from physics for these metaphysical echoes. In physics, 'remanence' refers to the residual magnetism in a medium once the magnetic field is removed. In dowsing, this idea is transposed to the remaining energy, of a residual stain that is left as a trace, trails where things have been moved, etheric traces of absent presences. It is these etheric melancholy moments which are captured in the work of British sculptor Rachel Whiteread. Through sculpting negative space, by taking casts of the interior of rooms, or even entire houses, Whiteread creates a type of 'lost object', a ghost of space. Freud's essay on *Mourning and Melancholia* described how the ego cannibalises or ingests the lost object, and this scenario seems played out in Whiteread's room casts, where the room itself has gone, in some cases demolished, but appears to have been absorbed by the remaining form. In the work *Ghost* (1990), Whiteread had the aim of 'mummifying the air in the room and making it solid', and created an 'afterlife' for an abandoned room from a terraced house in North London. Rachel Carley classified this particular kind of ghostly manifestation as a 'fetch', 'the ghost of someone living who is about to die'.[26]

Across London, another artist Rachel divined the remanence of another abandoned room. *Rodinsky's Room* is a project by artist Rachel Lichtenstein, recorded in a book written together with one of London's experts on 'museums of melancholy', Iain Sinclair.[27] Lichtenstein became obsessed with the room of David Rodinsky, a Jew who had lived above a synagogue in London's East End and disappeared in the 1960s. An iconic photograph of the room taken by Danny Gralton had captured the abandoned state of the room in a serene image, 'composed like a Vermeer painting, with a tactile quality that made the viewer want to reach out and touch the wallpaper so seductively dripping off the walls, that made the viewer gaze in wonder at the headline on a newspaper on the table, ISRAEL REBORN, perfectly positioned in the foreground. The light from the weaver's windows falling on the book-laden table added to the feeling that one was looking at an old Dutch masterpiece.'[28] This *vanitas*-like image fuelled Lichtenstein's curiosity, and was the beginning of an exhaustive process of research and investigation to unravel the mystery of Rodinsky. Working as artist, curator, researcher, Lichtenstein's life became focussed on Rodinsky and the book, *Rodinsky's Room,* itself became a portable museum of melancholy.

Rooms with the wallpaper dripping off, and the enigma of absent presences, pervade the work of photographer Francesca Woodman. The melancholy ambience of the photographs by Woodman, mostly of herself, is intensified with the realisation that she committed suicide at the age of just 22, in 1981. In the photographs Woodman often appears to be merging into the house itself, as though camouflaging herself. Reminiscent of the relationship between psychasthenia and the wish to disappear, as in the melancholy of clowns (Chapter 2), Woodman's work exhibits her being-seen-not-wanting-to-be-seen. She was often in motion in her work, and consequently appears slightly blurred; the resonances with the idea of a 'ghost' are chilling.[29] Woodman's photographs have an intense sense of memory, and a palpable presaging of her death.

Memory is also written into Tacita Dean's artworks, capturing the poignancy of abandoned places. In her film *Sound Mirrors* (1999), Dean recorded the acoustic mirrors on England's south coast. These large concrete structures were the pre-radar method of detecting enemies approaching, as the concave form concentrated the incoming sound waves to allow for monitoring, like huge concrete ears. Once at the cutting edge of technology in the 1930s, the acoustic mirrors were quickly abandoned with the advent of radars, and fell into ruin. Dean's film captures both the visual spectacle of decay and the aural emanations of these eerie ears. The melancholy of recent ruins was also the subject of her films, *Delft Hydraulics* (1996), which featured a machine for measuring wave impact which had been superseded by subsequent technologies, and *Bubble House* (1999), depicting a futuristic looking house, reminiscent of a flying saucer, in a state of abandonment.

In *The Russian Ending* Dean created an invented inventory of events. The melancholic iconography included images of explosions, shipwrecks and funerals, constructed from a series of second-hand, 'found' images.[30] Dean's works constructed the past, and blurred the boundary between documentation and fabrication. The postcard realities were made into large photogravure prints which were then glossed as faux film stills or treatments. At this point they received a second melancholic inflection, since the reference to the Russian ending recalls the age when films were made with alternative endings for different countries. Films made for American audiences had to end happily, while for Russians, a culture steeped in *toska*, they needed to end tragically.

Emptiness and Loneliness

The individual depicted as isolated, abandoned, apart, is often set against a landscape of loneliness – on the seashore as in the case of Edvard Munch's *Melancholia* (1902), or beneath the vaulted vastness of the night sky as in Anselm Kiefer's *Sternenfall* or 'Falling Stars' (1995). Kiefer's work is a kind of self portrait, a figure lying prone on very rough ground, staring at stars. There is an echo of what Cioran described as the interior and exterior boundlessness of melancholy, that 'interior infinitude… whose borders are ungraspable'.[31] And speaking of a later exhibition, also called 'Falling Stars', Kiefer explained, 'What you see is despair. I am completely desperate because I cannot explain why I am here. It's more than mourning, it's despair.'[32]

Pitting the self against the vastness of landscape emphasises the interior and exterior infinity, and is a compelling characteristic of the work of the nineteenth-century German Romantic painter, Caspar David Friedrich. Images like *The Abbey in the Oakwood* (1808–1810) are a litany of melancholy emblems, with Gothic ruins, dead trees, isolated figures, and a brooding, low-light sky. The bleak loneliness of the image runs through Friedrich's work, with the cool colour palette emphasising the ambience of isolation. Using colours like a ghostly blue, and green-black seas, the paintings have been described as having a similar mood to German Romantic musical compositions, an emphasis on the low strings. One of Friedrich's most palpably lonely images is *Monk by the Sea* (1808-1810), where the dark figure of a Capuchin monk stands at the edge of the sea, with a brooding sky above. Friedrich's contemporary, the German Romantic writer Kleist, conveys the lonely infinitude of this image: 'It is a wonderful thing to look out over an infinite watery waste, engulfed in an endless solitude at the seashore under a gloomy sky... the picture affects my heart, deeply moves me so that I become the Capuchin monk myself and the picture becomes the sand dune ... Nothing can be sadder and more uncomfortable than this position in the world. The only spark of life in the wide realm of death is the lonely central point in a lonely circle... like the apocalypse... boundlessness ... it has nothing but the frame for a foreground, it seems that when one looks at it it were as if one's eyelids were cut away...'[33]

Giorgio de Chirico's lonely melancholy is found in the city, where solitary figures, or more often only their shadows, glide through empty squares. The titles alone of de Chirico's works evoke the empty melancholy of the scene: *Melancholy and Mystery of a Street* (1914), *Nostalgia of the Infinite* (1911), and *The Melancholy of Departure* (1916). De Chirico's renderings of the Italian squares were often warped, subtly, by multiple perspective points to create an uneasy space, while the lighting of the late afternoon, near dusk, brings long shadows. Psychoanalysis of de Chirico's paintings has suggested many references to the loss of his father in phallic presences, seen in smoke stacks, columns, trains and bananas. This sense of loss, and its perpetuation, is quintessential Freudian melancholy, in distinction from mourning, a means of absorbing the loss and feeding off it. The images have also been diagnosed as being symptomatic of intestinal disorders,[34] migraine or epilepsy.[35] Notably these complaints are all associated with melancholia.

American painter Edward Hopper also excavated urban loneliness in paintings often populated by only one person, empty places, images of loss. Throughout his body of work Hopper's images are filled with loneliness, at the times of day which are most melancholy, the late afternoon with low glancing light, twilight, or night scenes lit to emphasise the sense of isolation. His image *Nighthawks* (1942) depicts four people in an American diner, in the dead of night. Each of the four is completely absorbed in their own introspection, and although they are physically present, there is instead an absent, empty feeling. The light spills out of the diner, a cool, unforgiving light. Basing the image on his own Manhattan neighbourhood, Hopper described it as 'painting the loneliness of a large city'.[36]

The emptiness of industrial areas, the wrecks and ruins, suggest a particular kind of melancholy, captured in the work of the German photographers, Bernd and Hiller Becher, and the Canadian, Edward Burtynsky. The Bechers pioneered the detached and stark photography of industrial buildings, their black and white images of the skeletal forms recording the structures as enigmatic icons of a passing age. Their photography has covered 50 years in the German industrial district, and occasionally further afield.[37] Their books, with titles including *Water Towers* (1988), *Gas Tanks* (1993), *Grain Elevators* (2006), and *Cooling Towers* (2006), suggest that species of melancholy which is characterised by the collector: the obsession with endless documentation, repetition.

Along the way Bernd Becher taught at the Düsseldorf Art Academy, where his students included Candida Höfer, Andreas Gursky, Thomas Ruff, and Thomas Struth, all of whom have continued to excavate melancholy from the everyday. Capturing the presence of absence, Höfer photographs places which are usually connected with intense human activity – the Louvre, libraries, factories – at times when they are empty.[38] Gursky's work amplifies the tedium of repetition in the everyday, evoking that Sisyphean species of melancholy, the ache of eternal recurrence. Vast facades of identical windows, views of cities, of the stockmarket, in which the melancholy sublimity is a culmination of many small elements combined.[39] The detached techniques of surveillance, as practised by the police during the German Autumn, inform the work of Thomas Ruff, including night shots of abandoned sites which look like 'crime scenes'.[40] Struth has also focused on empty streets, views of the most ordinary, regular and tedious parts of the urban fabric. As Guy Tosatto asks, 'Why these common buildings, these dull streets, these insignificant views? The question immediately gives way to an insistent melancholy, the melancholy associated with these familiar places whose strangeness and solitude are suddenly brought to light.'[41]

Like the presaging of a death, Edward Burtynsky recorded the preparations for the flooding of the Three Gorges in China, in what Carol Diehl called a 'photographic elegy'.[42] The poignant scenes of the cultural layer of the landscape being removed, and the realisation of what is imminent, are captured with an eerie fascination. Images of the impacts of mining, as seen in the devastated forest amidst uranium tailings in Elliot Lake, Ontario (1995), present a starkly poignant view of the landscape. Even in these sites of devastation, Burtynsky finds beauty, and this is the particular paradox of melancholy. Recalling the words of Edgar Allan Poe and Charles Baudelaire, both of whom found beauty in sorrow and death (see Chapter 1), the landscapes of Burtynsky's mines, quarries, and vast industrial infrastructure, assume this contradictory perception of beauty. His *Shipbreaking #8, Chittagong, Bangkok,* (2000)[43], for example, captures the scene of a watery landscape, with ruin-like elements. In the middle of it all, and barely discernible, are the figures of the labourers carrying out the dangerous task of breaking up the ships for scrap. The spectre of the 'heartless picturesque' looms in these images, these are the landscapes of 'heroin chic', the images which pose the moral question of finding beauty in landscapes that are built on suffering.

A Library of Melancholy Literature

As with any of the domains within this 'Blue Guide', the library of melancholy literature could fill a book on its own. The mind wanders first to the many icons of melan-

choly writing in the tradition of Romanticism and its al-
lies, Goethe's Werther[44] Chateaubriand's René[45], and
Pushkin's Onegin[46], are all exemplary melancholy char-
acters. The laments of Milton's *Il Penseroso* (1631),
Coleridge's *The Nightingale* (1798) and Keats's *Ode on
Melancholy* (1819), all converse with the melancholy of
nature, from Milton's 'arched walks of twilight groves, /
And shadows brown that Sylvan loves' to Coleridge's
'most melancholy bird', and Keats's 'sovran shrine of Veil'd
Melancholy'. Melancholy in nature is experienced as an
ultimate destination in James Beattie's *The Triumph of
Melancholy* (1760), where after wandering through many
affective states, the traveller yields at last to melancholy itself: 'Long I have laboured to elude thy sway! / But 'tis
enough, for I resist no more.'[47] Thomas Warton finds the
'chearless shades, / To ruin'd seats, to twilight cells and
bow'rs, / Where thoughtful Melancholy loves to muse /
Her favourite midnight haunts' in his *The Pleasures of
Melancholy* (1745).[48]

Taking it as read that such overtly melancholy classics
already have a place in this library, along with the various
works mentioned in passing through this book, the 'Blue
Guide' turns to some further thematic constellations of
ideas that inform the expression of melancholy. Three
clusters are explored: the hybrid form of literature which
includes found photographs or similar illustrations; a
metaphoric connection of city as self which explores the
exportation of ideas of melancholy to settings for novels;
and incomplete works which echo the impossible task of
the collector.

Photographic-literary works

As with the melancholy art exhibition sketched above, a library of melancholy might include works which emphasise aura and memory. The aura of the found photograph, as in the work of Gerhard Richter and Tacita Dean, is embedded within the writings of Georges Rodenbach, André Breton and WG Sebald, for example. Within these works, which hover between the autobiographical and the fictional, the use of ambiguous images infuses the writing with a melancholy weightiness. The books are steeped in memories, of recollected journeys on foot, through the city of Bruges for Rodenbach, Paris for Breton, and along the South Coast of England and through Germany for Sebald. These memories are constructed and/or re-constructed with the help of the monochromatic images. The often poor quality of these photographs embodies a feeling of nostalgia and the images are sometimes uncaptioned, unassigned, with no indication of their provenance.

Bruges-la-Morte is the title of Rodenbach's novel – 'Bruges-the-Dead' – and the combination of melancholy text and sombre images creates a profound sense of a mourning city. The images, which are mostly anonymous postcards or stock views, are almost completely devoid of people, and in some cases the figures have been cut out of the pictures. There is a mood of eerie silence and stillness, and the views are stage-managed by the author so that this version of Bruges resists any familiar connections that might undo the weight of his text. The text is suffused with a bleak atmosphere, and the photographs reinforce the idea of *memento mori*, reminders of death, the central theme of the novel.

In André Breton's *Nadja*, photographs of Paris are interspersed in the text, along with other graphic material, including drawings, pages of handwriting, and engravings. Like Bruges in Rodenbach's images, Breton's Paris is mostly vacant, or certainly empty of the events to which the narrative alludes. The scene of a dinner outside the City Hotel is poignantly deserted, and the image which relates to a remembered walk through the Tuileries Gardens together is similarly desolate. The photographs are not always anonymous and, in fact, some are attributed to fellow surrealist, Man Ray. The images in the book are captioned and recorded in a list of illustrations, which lends them a certain 'authenticity.' Yet, they hover at the edge of reality since, although 'autobiographical', it is not clear when Breton's *Nadja* slides into fiction. The captions apprehend the images and coerce them into the story. The art of the readymade is again at play and, in this case, it is the act of captioning which elevates the sometimes seemingly trivial images into elements of significance. The drawings are done by Nadja, the seductive and elusive central figure of Breton's tale, adding a layer of poignancy to the work. Nadja is seemingly suffering from schizophrenia, and ends up in a lunatic asylum. Breton's indifference to all of this, despite his attraction to her, brings again the spectre of a heartless form of aesthetic, of finding beauty because of, or in spite of, the suffering of others. The closing passages of Nadja emphasise this contradictory form of melancholy aesthetic, 'Beauty is like a train that ceaselessly roars out of the Gare de Lyon and which I know will never leave, which has not left', and in Breton's famous mantra which closes the book: 'Beauty will be CONVULSIVE or will not be at all.'[49]

Enigmatic and elusive, the images in WG Sebald's novels convey a curious quality, almost like stills drawn somewhat arbitrarily from a film. Some resonate strongly with the text, as in *The Rings of Saturn*, where a *vanitas*-like photograph of a skull sitting on a small pile of books appears amidst the passage on Thomas Browne, author of *Urn Burial*.[50] By implication this is Browne's skull, since Sebald is relating the tale of how Browne's skull and a lock of his hair had been left firstly to a parish councillor and then to the hospital museum, where they were displayed under a bell jar. Yet the image does not show a skull under a bell jar, so the enigma persists, and eludes capture, while at the same time adding a weighty, melancholic gravitas to the text. At times the images ground the text, when a direct reference is made to a photograph, such as, for example, the photograph of Sebald himself in *The Rings of Saturn,* where he leans against a Lebanese cedar at Ditchingham. This is part of a lament for the loss of trees to old age and disease, which proceeds in the pages either side, and which is supported by a further photograph of a forlorn field filled with dead and dying poplars.[51] All of this is also foreshadowing a certain end to many of the other trees, as it was in the period preceding the hurricanes that swept through south-east England in 1987.

In addition to the photographs with their auratic, nostalgic mood, there are also fragments of diagrams and paintings punctuating Sebald's novels. In *The Emigrants* there is a hand-drawn diagram of a railway station, as well as family photographs, photographs of unspecified places, and a copy of pages from a diary.[52] *Vertigo* includes advertisements, Sebald's passport, a train ticket, fragments from Giotto's frescoes, a page from a calendar, all of which serve variously to support the text or to act in seeming independence of it.[53] Their 'readymade' nature infuses them with a surreal quality, such that even the most banal and quotidian qualities are elevated to something somehow mystical and significant.

City as Self

Melancholy distinguished itself from the other humoral types in many ways, one of which was that it became a quality that was not only found in people but also was recognisable in landscapes of all types, including urban areas. There are resonances between the melancholy of the self and that of the city, for example, and a number of authors make this explicit, forming a particular constellation of melancholy literature. This type of metaphorical connection is an echo of Sigmund Freud's conception of Rome as a model of the human mind. Rome's layers upon layers of urban development were, Freud prognosed, similar to memory. His analogy is ambiguous, however, as he pointed out that if Rome was in fact a human mind, a 'psychical entity', rather than a built form, 'Where the Coliseum stands now we could at the same time admire Nero's Golden House; on the Piazza of the Pantheon we should find not only the Pantheon of today as bequeathed to us by Hadrian, but on the same site also Agrippa's original edifice; indeed, the same ground would support the church of Santa Maria sopra Minerva and the old temple over which it was built.'[54] So, although the city might be like the mind in the way it gathers up layers of memory, it is also unlike the mind as some parts are demolished and rebuilt; everything doesn't co-exist. Despite this ambiguity, the resonances between the city and self remain a powerful metaphor, and one that has particular potency with the exporting of the idea of melancholy to the urban fabric.

Orhan Pamuk's *Istanbul* is an extensive meditation on the soul of that city, in the peculiarly Turkish melancholy of *hüzün* – of the 'feeling that the city of Istanbul carries as its fate'.[55]   It is in the passage on the *hüzün* embedded in the iconic black and white films set in the city that there are strong echoes of a Freudian investment of the self in the city. Pamuk recalls that in these films the anguish of a heart-broken hero comes not from the individual himself, but 'it is almost as if the *hüzün* which infuses the city's sights and streets and famous views has seeped into the hero's heart to break his will. It then seems that to know the hero's story and share his melancholy I need only to look at the view.'[56] For, it is in the view that one finds either the brooding presence of the Bosphorus, or the back street ruins, and there is that sense, in Istanbul, of it all being there at once, very much in the manner of Freud's hypothetical version of Rome.

Hugues, the main character from Rodenbach's *Bruges-la-Morte,* relates how he selected the city of Bruges as a home because of its melancholy. He explains that 'cities especially have a personality, an autonomous spirit, an almost externalized character corresponding to joy, to new love, to renunciation, to widowerhood. Every city is a state of mind, and one hardly needs to stay there for this state of mind to communicate itself, to spread to us in a fluid that inoculates and that one incorporates with the nuance of the air.'[57] Hugues' relationship with the city as cipher of the self is circular, as he grows unlike the city for a time, when he finds a new relationship with which he tries to overcome the grief of the death of his wife. Eventually the relationship fails, and he becomes once more like the city, 'finding himself again the brother in silence and melancholy of this mournful Bruges, this *soror dolorosa* [sad sister]. How right he had been to come there at the time of his great grief! Mute analogies!'[58]

Joris-Karl Huysmans' *Against Nature* (1884), Gustave Flaubert's *November* (1910), and Jean-Paul Sartre's *Nausea* (1938), all exhibit the *ennui* of the self in the city, with all three central characters battling with their relationship with their broader setting. Their melancholy is the core of their being, as in Flaubert's nameless narrator who declares, 'If you had asked me what it was I needed, I wouldn't have been able to tell you; my desires had no specific object, and my sadness had no immediate cause; or rather, there were so many objects and so many causes that I wouldn't have been able to isolate a single one of them.'[59] Huysman's central character, Des Esseintes, had found 'hatching in the dismal forcing-house of *ennui*, the frightening climacteric of thoughts and emotions'.[60] He had a figure of *Melancholia* which he treated almost like a religious icon, and would spend hours meditating in front of it. The central characters of all three novels suffer from *ennui*, and various related melancholic feelings, effecting a melancholic camouflage with their contexts, so that the city and the self begin to melt together. Flaubert's nameless narrator has a hatred of being 'jostled by the crowd', feeling like a 'wild beast tracked down in its lair'.[61] And in Sartre's *Nausea*, Roquentin expresses all of the melancholy that comes from disenchantment with the world, the tedium, the bourgeoisie, and the very nature of existence itself.

Des Esseintes, Flaubert's 'I', and Roquentin, all want to disappear, to become camouflaged, the melancholy ploy of not wanting to be seen. Flaubert's character struggled with the 'restless surge of wicked, cowardly, idiotic and ugly men'. Being part of this crowd brought him anguish, the feeling of being 'like a piece of seaweed swept along by the ocean, lost in the midst of the numberless waves that rolled and roared on every side of me.'[62] This tension of being part of the masses, yet not wanting to be there, or being like seaweed, echoes with Caillois' psychasthenia, of the act of camouflage, with particular resonance with 'the fish Phyllopteryx, from the Sargasso Sea, [which] is simply "torn seaweed in the shape of floating strands"'[63]. As outlined in Chapter 2, the strategies of camouflage are often more revealing than concealing, so at the same time as attempting to disappear one can become even more obvious than before.

There are echoes still of the humoral tradition, and the relationship to the physiology and seasonal metaphors of melancholy. Flaubert's character's *November* is the fear of having reached a premature *autumn*, that very point upon the ancient constellation of melancholy. Des Esseintes also gravitates to autumn, in his recognition of how Baudelaire had 'laid bare the morbid psychology of the mind that has reached the October of its sensations, and had listed the symptoms of souls visited by sorrow, singled out by spleen'.[64] Rodenbach's Hugues is also drawn to the melancholy moment of the city, setting out for his 'usual twilight stroll, despite the relentless late autumn drizzle, shedding tears, weaving into the water, tacking the air, pricking the still surface of the canals, capturing and paralysing the soul like a bird trapped in the wet meshes of an endless net.'[65]

The characters evoked by Flaubert, Huysmans, and Sartre, all share the sensation of 'nausea', and it is significant that Sartre's book of that name was originally titled *Melancholia*, emphasising the root of this mood of revulsion of the self in relation to the milieu. The characters suffer a feeling of claustrophobia brought about by the paradox of camouflage, of the struggle to exist, yet not exist. A melancholy born of the boredom of the age, and of that conundrum that has persisted for two and a half millennia: fear and sadness *without cause*. This conflicted existence was also captured in Søren Kierkegaard's *Either/Or:A Fragment of Life,* where the young aesthete is, as translator Alastair Hannay puts it, 'the modern hero, richly egocentric, tragically melancholic, excitingly nihilistic, daringly imaginative'.[66] And Flaubert's narrator has that very mood of a masochistic enjoyment of the condition of ongoing sadness:'I am just amazed that there is still room in my heart for suffering; but man's heart is an inexhaustible reservoir of melancholy: one or two moments of happiness fill it to the brim, but all the many miseries of humanity can easily congregate and find lodgings in it together.'[67]

Nausea is a symptom associated with 'hypochondriacal melancholy', another of which is vertigo, according to Robert Burton's sixteenth-century *Anatomy of Melancholy.* And *Vertigo* is the title of another melancholy investigation of the self in space, the work of WG Sebald. In one passage Sebald navigates the anguish of the self in the city, of how there is 'something peculiarly dispiriting about the emptiness that wells up when, in a strange city, one dials the same telephone numbers in vain. If no one answers, it is a disappointment of huge significance, quite as if these few random ciphers were a matter of life or death. So what else could I do, when I had put the coins that jingled out of the box back into my pocket, but wander aimlessly around until well into the night.' He relates the onset of paranoia, the hallucinations which follow him in the city, of the vision of Dante walking a short distance ahead of him, 'with the familiar cowl on his head, distinctly taller than the people in the street, yet he passed by them unnoticed. When I walked faster in order to catch him up he went down Heinrichsgasse, but when I reached the corner he was nowhere to be seen. After one or two turns of this kind I began to sense in me a vague apprehension, which manifested itself as a feeling of vertigo.'[68]

Roquentin's nausea has a similarly paranoiac sense, and his relationship with his surroundings disturbed him: 'The Nausea is not inside me: I feel it out there in the wall, in the suspenders, everywhere around me. It makes itself one with the café, I am the one who is within it.' The city echoes this melancholic alienation, a place where, 'I can't feel myself any longer; I am won over by the purity surrounding me; nothing is alive, the wind whistles, straight lines flee in the night. The boulevard Noir doesn't have the indecent look of bourgeois streets, which try to charm the passers-by: it is simply a reverse side... The boulevard Noir is inhuman. Like a mineral. Like a triangle... Straight, dirty corridors, with a howling draught and wide, treeless pavements. The[se boulevards] are almost always outside the town in those strange districts where cities are manufactured, near goods stations, tram depots, slaughter-houses, and gasometers... The Nausea has stayed over there, in the yellow light.'[69]

The Incomplete

Incompletion is a melancholy trait, reflecting the deferral of closure, and is manifested in unfinished books. In *The Rings of Saturn* WG Sebald describes the work of nineteenth-century writer Edward FitzGerald, who was at times afflicted by what he called the 'blue devil of melancholy'.[70] FitzGerald inhabited a hermitage for a period and worked on introspective projects – extensive correspondence, and making notes towards a 'dictionary of commonplaces', constructing a glossary of nautical terms, and also a Sévigné dictionary referencing the corpus of correspondence by Madame de Sévigné. This project, like all of his others remained incomplete.

Another literary lacuna is Gustave Flaubert's *Dictionary of Received Ideas,* a collection of clichés and platitudes, intended to illustrate idiocy. This in itself is a boundless enterprise, and could go on forever, so it is not surprising that it remains in incomplete form amongst Flaubert's oeuvre. It is a companion piece to the novel *Bouvard and Pécuchet,* the story of two copy-clerks who give up their day jobs to pursue their interest in the world of ideas. Amongst the entries in the ambitious and unfinishable dictionary of idiocy is 'melancholy': 'Sign of a noble heart and a lofty mind.'[71]

The Sisyphean task of the lexicographer, the encyclopaedist, is illustrated by Reşat Ekrem Koçu, author of the *Istanbul Encyclopedia.* After toiling for nearly 30 years Koçu finished his eleventh volume, having reached the letter G. It had taken him from 1944 to 1951 just to get from A to B, in some 1,000 pages, documenting what he referred to as 'Strange and Curious Facts from Our History'. Orhan Pamuk casts Koçu as one of the '*hüzün*-drenched souls who helped create an image of a twentieth-century Istanbul as a half-finished city afflicted with melancholy'.[72] The not even half-finished encyclopedia is thus a metaphor for the city at large.

Some works remain incomplete because of the author's demise, others because they are unfinishable since they deal with infinitudes, and a third species are written to be incomplete. This last ploy is a means of achieving a melancholy delay in resolution, of unsettling the text. Italo Calvino's *If On a Winter's Night a Traveller* does just this, and evades a sense of ever finishing the book, of being able to put it aside. Within the novel are ten incomplete novel fragments, all of which are of distinct genres. While on one level an iconic post-modern manoeuvre, it also achieves a sense of gravitas, since each incomplete novel contains a fragment of one sentence, which embodies a moment of melancholy: 'If on a winter's night a traveller, outside the town of Malbork, leaning from the steep slope without fear of wind or vertigo, looks down in the gathering shadow in a network of lines that enlace, in a network of lines that intersect, on the carpet of leaves illuminated by the moon around an empty grave – What story down there awaits its end?'[73]

A Melancholy Playlist

Robert Burton in *The Anatomy of Melancholy* made the prognosis that, 'Many men are melancholy by hearing Musick, but it is a pleasing melancholy that it causeth, and therefore to such as are discontent, in woe, fear, sorrow or dejected it is a most present remedy; it expels care, alters their grieved minds and easeth in an instant.'[74] Music and melancholy are potent partners. Around the seventeenth century melancholy took its 'poetic' turn, and became an enhanced self-awareness, a heightened sensibility. One of the key shifts at the time was the role of music – not as an antidote to pathological melancholy, a cure or therapy but, as Klibansky, Panofsky and Saxl describe it, 'to soothe and at the same time nourish this ambiguous bitter-sweet mood'.[75]

The connections of music and memory are strong, and a remembered piece of music acts as a compelling memory trigger. Music, in this sense, is the locus of nostalgia, and an often personal sphere of melancholy, a connection to life events, recollections of moments in time. Music can also evoke melancholy beyond the personal, into a collective response to something as simple as the sound of an instrument, or as complex as the content of the lyrics.

Certain musical instruments seem naturally to elicit a sense of melancholy. The piano accordion's nostalgic East European tones, or the plaintive strains of a violin, for example, or Chinese instruments like the two-stringed violin-like *erhu*, or bamboo flute, the *dizi,* with their fragile notes suffused with melancholic tone. The sound of whistling, as in Goldfrapp's track 'Lovely Head' from the album *Felt Mountain* (2000), or a violin, as in the deliciously poignant instrumental, 'Fawn', on Tom Waits's album *Alice* (2002). The Armenian double-reed instrument, the *duduk,* which has a haunting, ghostly sound, the 'combination of an alto clarinet, a Gypsy violin and a contralto's sigh',[76] or the bagpipes, with their melody offset by the brooding drone, which in the tradition of the Irish were used to 'accompany their dead to the grave, making such mournful sounds as to invite, nay almost force the bystanders to weep'.[77]

Many cultures have a traditional style of melancholy music, in the form of laments, love songs, and ballads. The *enka* style of music developed in 1860s Japan, the first time the Japanese pentatonic scale was blended with Western musical scales, and is a particularly emotional style of singing. *Enka* singers use a vibrato singing technique and their formal performances in traditional dress have become reservoirs of Japanese nostalgia and identity. Like those of the Portuguese *fado* or the Greek *rebetika*, *enka* lyrics relate stories of suffering, love, and death. The *saudade* of the *fado* is echoed in the *duende* of the Spanish *flamenco*. Federico García Lorca, in his passionate description of *duende*, located this deep, brooding melancholy within the *flamenco* singing of Manuel Torre. On hearing another singer perform his flamenco work *Nocturno de Generalife*, Torre declared, 'All that has black sounds has *duende*.'[78] *Duende's* dark melancholy is also found in the Argentinean *tango*, traditionally played on the guitar, violin and flute, and later by the iconic *bandoneón*, the button accordion. Developed by European immigrants in the early twentieth century, Argentinean *tango* expresses a romantic melancholy of fatalism and love. Crossing the world to Finland, the *tango* took on a new cultural overlay, with the different melancholy sense of *kaiho*, of loneliness and longing.

Within the vast realm of classical music there are numerous melancholy works. From the early moments of Western classical music, melancholy is there in the religious music of Hildegard of Bingen. Hildegard saw music as a type of therapy for those afflicted with melancholy, and also a vehicle for conveying her ideas, as in *Ordo Virtutum*, the 'Order of the Virtues' (1151). The dark species of religious melancholy, the enduring of suffering, permeates JS Bach's *St Matthew Passion* (1728), of which the aria 'Erbame dich mein Gott' is an extraordinarily moving and evocative musical passage, with a solo violin and vocalist singing the text which translates as, 'Have mercy, my God / for the sake of my tears'. The aria was used by Tarkovsky as the opening for his final film *The Sacrifice,* where it accompanies an equally moving visual, as the camera pans slowly across Leonardo da Vinci's *Adoration of the Magi.*

The brooding melancholy of death haunts the funeral marches of Grieg and Wagner, and Handel's 'Dead March' from his *Saul* opera (1738). Chopin's 'Death March' and his 'Waltz no. 7' are extremely redolent melancholy pieces. In evoking the sense of *toska,* Russian political prisoner AS Arzhilovsky explained how it was captured within this piece of Chopin's, recalling how, 'Misha played two waltzes by Chopin, and I broke down in tears. The sounds of the immortal composer just scraped my soul. His waltz no. 7 is full of tender sadness, full of deep tenderness for the irretrievable past. I long to put this into words, every note is so dear to me, so much a part of my long-suffering soul.'[79] Chopin's contemporary, Beethoven, writes his own suffering into his work, most notably in the movement 'Malincolia' from the Quartet op. 18, No. 6 and the 'Largo' of the Piano Sonata op.10, No.3, which was explained by Beethoven himself as the 'description of the state of mind of a melancholic'.[80]

The German sense of *wehmut* is found in the work of Gustav Mahler, from the German-speaking former Austrian Empire. His *Symphony No. 9* (1909-1910) is one of the most melancholy works, written after learning that his wife had been unfaithful, which evoked his motif of 'death in the midst of life'. The excavation of the melancholy from earlier religious music was the foundation of the early work of French composer Erik Satie. His enigmatically titled *Gymnopédies* (1888) and *Gnossiennes* (1890) have a strongly melancholic atmosphere. The *Gymnopédies,* for example, make reference to ancient Greece, and the practice of gymnastic exercises, and were described as having an 'antique flavour' with phrases floating 'mournfully over a slow pulsing bass', inhabited by a 'shadow show' and 'phantom figures'.[81] Satie's music is characterised by repetition, the Sisyphean aspect of melancholy, and his original intention was that the music was to be a mere background – what he called 'furniture music'.

Modern minimalist classical composers also mined earlier sacred music as sources for melancholy, as in the work of Arvo Pärt, Henryk Górecki and Giya Kancheli. Estonian minimalist Pärt's work resonates with medieval sources, and conveys a search for the numinous, the holy other, that which is sacred and beyond the known. Pärt describes how rather than seeking 'colour', he 'draws with black and white'.[82] One of Pärt's musical expressions was what he called 'tintinnabulation', or a bell-like sound, as in his *Passo Domini nostri Jesu Christi secumdum Joannem,* which produces an indefinable melancholy.[83] Górecki, from Poland, is also a 'sacred minimalist', and his best-known work is the Third Symphony, the *Symphony of Sorrowful Songs,* in which the slowly paced music is accompanied by three melancholy texts: a lament from the fifteenth century, the writings of a teenage prisoner in a Gestapo prison cell, and a folk song. The spiritual works of Belgium-based Georgian composer Kancheli are characterised by silences and sounds that have an aura, paralleling that which is effected by a reduction of technology. His *Svietlaya piechal* ('Light Sorrow' or 'Sweet Sadness') is a piece that dwells on silence or near-silence, and John Cage described it as a 'work of innocence' and noted how the boys' voices effected 'the absence of technology'. Kancheli himself wrote how he 'wanted the voices of children to remind us of angels we have never heard... The piece is dedicated to the memory of children killed in World War II.'[84]

The melancholy of music, then, has an extensive history, ranging from the traditional instruments and forms of music to the vast classical canon. Within all of these two main forces are at work – form and content. 'Formal' aspects include those elements which affect the shape of music, its tempo, texture, timbre, while the effects of content are derived through the lyrical components, or the referencing to other familiar fragments of music in the form of a 'quotation' or 'sample'.

Formal manoeuvres that bring about a mood of melancholy often build upon an idea of defamiliarisation, or *ostranenie*. A theory developed by the Russian Formalists, in particular Viktor Shklovsky, this was a means of altering the apprehension of that which has become habitual.[85] Ways of defamiliarising or 'making strange' include the practices of placing things in different contexts (such as the readymade), or changing them in some way, altering their colour or texture, or somehow subverting the way in which a work is encountered. In melancholy music this might be achieved by a shift in tempo. For example, Kancheli's *Life without Christmas* is an exceptionally slow piece of music, which Susan Bradshaw suggests is exceeded only by Olivier Messiaen's *Quatuor pour le Fin du Temps,* the 'Quartet for the End of Time'[86] – a tempo which is described as 'infinitely slow'.[87]

The process of slowing down is entwined within the idea of defamiliarisation, as the belief was that, if the apprehension of the art is 'retarded' or slowed down, it can be better appreciated. This resonates strongly with the needs of melancholy, which 'hates haste', and the feeling that, as in nostalgia, things are recollected out of time, out of place. In music, defamiliarisation through altering tone and texture can have a potent melancholy value. In composing the music for Bill Morrison's film *Decasia,* Michael Gordon sought to bypass the way in which music is habitually received. Instead he aspired to achieve 'the equivalent of the look of decayed celluloid in music'.[88] In his mind there was an image of a piano which had been sitting untuned for 100 years, and these notional untuned pianos can be heard on the score. The orchestra itself is detuned, so that they play ⅛th of a tone higher or lower, to convey the sense of imprecision and instability.

Detuning was a technique used on the Smashing Pumpkins' album, *Mellon Collie and the Infinite Sadness* (1995). The central theme of the album was of life and death, and of the human condition, particularly the pervasive sense of sorrow. A wide variety of instruments is used on the album, including such 'low-tech' effects as salt shakers and scissors, but significantly it was the guitars which added the overarching melancholy effect. By tuning all the guitars down half a step the overall mood of the music is lower, with an enhanced sense of gravity. The guitars were also put in a dropped D tuning on some tracks, which has an added melancholy value.

A dropped D tuning detunes the bottom string from E down to D, meaning it is possible to play in the key of D with a lower bass tonic, or key note of the chord, than normally possible with standard tuning. This gives the effect of a 'drone'. There are further variations of this, as in the double dropped D tuning which means the top string is also tuned down to D, and it is this tuning which gives the poignant feel of The Doors' 'The End' (1967). A variation of the dropped D tuning is the shift to D minor, as in Skip James's intensely poignant 'Hard Time Killing Floor' (1931), which expressed the anguish of depression times, and featured in the Coen Brothers' film *O Brother Where Art Thou* (2000).

While the range of formal manoeuvres can alter the way in which music is received, overlaying it with a melancholy ambience, the content of music is also a bearer of melancholy. Lyrics can embed melancholy into music, from the heart-rending songs of Country and Western music, to the ache of the Blues; or in the writings of the 'messiah of melancholy', *The Cure's* Robert Smith; or the lyrical melancholy genius of 'American Troubadour', Bob Dylan. The melancholy of lyrics is more akin to the literary tradition, as a form of poetry, like the troubadours and balladeers of the past, and there are two contemporary poets who convey distinctive melancholic types – Tom Waits and Nick Cave.

Tom Waits is the Edward Hopper of lyric writing. Called the 'prince of melancholy' by film director Francis Ford Coppola, Waits comes from California and recorded his first album in 1973. From that first album, *Closing Time,* he has conjured up the imagery of the melancholy margins of American society. During his early years this reflected a world, very familiar to him, of 'drunks, hookers, petty thieves, small-town refugees, greasy dives, all-night drives, used car lots, hotel shootouts'. Where singers like Bruce Springsteen sing about such characters, 'Waits sings as one'.[89] The echoes with Hopper's imagery are amplified in the name of his 1975 album, *Nighthawks at the Diner* – the title of Edward Hopper's painting from 1942. From the poignant love-songs, as in those written for Coppola's *One from the Heart,* to the sketches of the low-life world and shadowy streets, a deep mood of melancholy percolates through Waits' music, like the vision conjured up by his 'Nighthawk Postcards':

There's a blur drizzle down the plateglass
as a neon swizzle stick stirrin' up the sultry night air
and a yellow biscuit of a buttery cue ball moon
rollin' maverick across an obsidian sky[90]

The visions of memory and nostalgia suffuse the lyrics, aided by the accompaniments like the violin, accordion, or even a calliope – a steam organ. The poetry of the lyrics set the scene for such melancholy moments, as in 'Barcarolle':

And the train whistle blows
And the carnival goes
Till there's only the tickets and crows here
And the grass will all grow back[91]

Nick Cave's melancholy is of a different flavour, coloured with the anguish of centuries of religious and love melancholy. England-based Australian Cave's lyrics have strong connections to the lengthy genealogy of melancholy. In 'The Song of Joy', for example, a ballad which circles around how 'all things move toward their end', there is a line ('No wonder', people said, 'poor mother Joy's so melancholy'[92]) which seems to reach back through the centuries to lines from Burton's seventeenth-century *Anatomy of Melancholy*: 'A thousand pleasures do me bless, / And crown my soule with happiness / All my joyes besides are folly, / None so sweet as melancholy.'[93]

Cave's lyrics echo the angst of the Desert Fathers, with their apprehension about Christ's presence in their world, the melancholy of *deus absconditus*. St John of the Cross even makes a cameo appearance in one of Cave's songs, 'There She Goes, My Beautiful World', which recalls how 'St. John of the Cross did his best stuff imprisoned in a box'[94], a reference to his time of imprisonment in a cell, during which he wrote *Dark Night of the Soul*. Love and religion are tightly entwined in Cave's music, with the 'actualising of God' coming through the medium of the love song, in a way which is often ambiguous, such that the songs might be sung either to God or to a romantic love interest.[95] At other times, the lyrics seem to make a direct appeal, and express the distress of religious anguish, as in the track 'Oh My Lord':

Oh Lord, Oh my Lord
Oh Lord
How have I offended thee?

Wrap your tender arms around me
Oh Lord, Oh Lord
Oh My Lord[96]

Cave declared, 'The love song must resonate with the susurration of sorrow, the tintinnabulation of grief.'[87] Cave's profound attention to melancholy is reinforced in almost prayer-like or liturgical litanies, lists of travesties and agonies, as in 'People Ain't No Good', with its plea:

To our love send a dozen white lilies
To our love send a coffin of wood
To our love let all the pink-eyed pigeons coo
That people they just ain't no good
To our love send back all the letters
To our love a valentine of blood
To our love let all the jilted lovers cry
That people they just ain't no good[98]

The melancholy mode of repetition is also expressed in the obsession with a single object of desire, as in the mantra uttered over and over in 'Black Hair':

Full of all my whispered words, her black hair
And wet with tears and good-byes, her hair of
    deepest black
All my tears cried against her milk-white throat
Hidden behind the curtain of her beautiful black
    hair[99]

The Architecture and Landscape of Sadness

As part of the contemporary obsession with eliminating sadness, architecture and the designed landscape aspire to the state of an untroubled paradise. The advertising material for new housing developments, condominiums, and parks is dominated by images of sunlit scenes, trees, water, moments of Arcadia. Alain de Botton's book *The Architecture of Happiness*[100] in its title alone asserts a certain perspective on ideals for the built environment. While what Botton is advocating is more complex than an un-qualified 'happiness', and might instead be called a feeling of wellbeing, it does signal a particular preoccupation in contemporary society. Wellbeing is, after all, a condition of balance, one that also requires sadness. As theologian Thomas Moore warns, 'If we do away with Saturn's dark moods, we may find it exhausting trying to keep life bright and warm at all costs. We may be even more over-come then by increased melancholy called forth by the repression of Saturn, and lose the sharpness and substance of identity that Saturn gives the soul.'[101]

Searching for an architecture of melancholy is fraught with pitfalls. The heartless picturesque always lurks nearby, deriving aesthetic pleasure from the suffering of others. In the context of the designed environment – i.e. archi-tecture and landscape architecture – could this mean that poorly designed places could be sources of melancholy? After all, they are often sites of suffering, the contempo-rary version of Will Fern's hovel in *The Chimes*. A useful distinction is found in Susan Sontag's words: 'Depression is melancholy minus its charms – the animation, the fits.'[102] Although writing about a mental state, Sontag's description could apply to the designed environment, where sad buildings, sad parks, are nothing more than depressive because of their poor design, their bad lighting, and their spatial dysfunctionality. Such places are not melancholy, they are simply depressing.

Beyond the fascination with the black melancholy of the heartless picturesque, the noble picturesque also persists in landscapes ravaged by time and poverty. In his honouring of his native Istanbul, Orhan Pamuk captures such a vision. From the outset, with an epigraph by writer Ahmet Rasim ('The beauty of a landscape resides in its melancholy'[103]), Pamuk traces the way in which the city's past is suffused in the collective melancholy of the people – in the Turkish melancholy of *hüzün*. Although it is also the stain of a great deal of suffering, the melancholy is received with a sense of grace and poignancy, rather than the detached pleasure of the ladies drawing Will Fern's hovel in their sketchbooks.

While it is important that architecture and landscape can elicit positive, 'happy' feelings, there needs to be places to feel sorrow. Churches and cemeteries provide formalised settings for grief, mourning and contemplation, but beyond such places there are other sites which might be sought out for their melancholy. Places like the retreat described by John Evelyn, writing of a space made for solace and meditation: '… I made… the stews & receptacles for Fish, and built a little study over a cascade, to passe my Melancholy hours shaded there with Trees, & silent enough…'[104]   Where, then, should the 'Blue Guide' plot places of melancholy? The silent places of memory, ruins, darkness and shadows.

Memory

The melancholy of memorials is perhaps, at first, an obvious connection. As markers of things lost they are the archetypical apparatus of grief. But memorials can become 'invisible' and fail in their melancholic potential. Through the use of clichéd forms – the man-on-a-podium, for example – they fail to become effective, affective moments in the landscape, to trigger an emotional response. Other memorials fail through their efforts to 'close the wound', to create a sense of completion at the site of tragedy. One of the primary ways this is done is through a type of memorial arithmetic, with the attention focussed on numbers, how many dead, the date, the time. Arguably such 'data' can objectify the nature of loss, through denaturing it, turning it into mere numbers, in order to bring resolution and an end to grief. Yet, if sites of memory simply become tick-boxes, how might they move the beholders, to appreciate the tragic, to experience melancholy? The 'Blue Guide' seeks out those memorials which transcend the landscape wallpaper of statues and plinths, and strives to look beyond the tidy logic of numbers and dates.

Some of the most melancholy memorials are those which do not say much at all, leaving the viewer to make an effort, to become part of it, and to consequently form an affective bond. These memorials are not simply objects, but experiences. They invite participation rather than mere observance. The point is not seeking to find a 'cure' for grief, but accepting that sorrow is a necessary component of our human condition. Sometimes the experience may hang over the visitor like a question mark, something unsolvable, beyond comprehension, a wound kept open through the work of the memorial. The Vietnam Veterans' Memorial (1982) in Washington DC, designed by architect and sculptor Maya Lin, effects such a sense of the ineffable, the unspeakable, through a form which is a metaphorical gash, an opening in the ground. Lin's memorial design challenged all that had gone before, providing the antithesis of a figure on a podium, instead pushing a memorial wall down into the ground, a wall that is incised with the names of over 58,000 American servicemen dead or missing in action. The question of how a visitor might sense grief at the loss of people not known to them, what Rico Franses calls the 'stranger memorial', is central to the nature of melancholy.[105] The 'lost object' of melancholy is not necessarily a known person or thing, but something far less tangible. A site that remembers 'strangers' can become such an intangibility, and the melancholy is imbued by the more universal apprehension of death, love and loss.

Two extended sets of memorials provide some of the most melancholy markers of loss. Memorials to the Jewish Holocaust and to the Irish Potato Famine can be found at far flung points of the globe. Two recent Jewish Holocaust memorials provide places of suspended grief through their abstraction of the magnitude of loss. The challenge of providing a setting for the memory of such an event is one which pushes design to its limits. Literary theorist Terry Eagleton suggested that such was the enormousness of this tragedy that it 'beggar[ed] representation' and the 'only appropriate response would be screaming or silence'.[106] To effect a design equivalent of such a response is to find the profound space of melancholy, one which architect Peter Eisenman sought through an obstinately abstract memorial in Berlin, near the Brandenburg Gate. The Memorial to the Murdered Jews of Europe (2004) is obstinate because it resists symbolism, it rejects an easy slide into closure, and instead the 2,711 concrete stelae, vertical rectangular forms, stand for something ineffable, something beyond the symbolic, things that are beyond reason. A second example is the Garden of Stones (2003) at New York's Museum of Jewish Heritage, by the British sculptor, Andy Goldsworthy. Despite efforts to derive the symbolism in Goldsworthy's work, to say what the stones 'mean', to count them, to reduce them to figures, the memorial is at its most powerful when considered as an abstract expression of something beyond a ready reduction to facts and figures. The large stones sit on a terrace which projects from the museum, with their bulky forms appearing somehow uncanny in the space, unexpected. This unease is deepened by the appearance of small trees growing out of the tops of each stone, a contradiction, a resistance to an 'easy reading' of the complexity of memory.

Not far from the Garden of Stones in New York is artist Brian Tolle's Irish Hunger Memorial, one of over 30 memorials to this tragedy around the globe. Again it uses the motif of stones, but in this case they are explicitly symbolic, referring to the Irish counties, and also take the form of a recreated Irish cottage as a ruin. The memorial uses sound as well, through playing recordings of narration of diary entries that recount the experience of the famine. The strongly scripted nature of the memorial, in terms of its orchestration of the visitor's experience, can detract from the gravity of grief, and the melancholy is most palpable beyond the script, when the austerity of the ruined cottage or the vertiginous edge of the memorial, which juts out into space towards the Hudson River, can be contemplated and when it is allowed to remain unresolved. At the Hyde Park Barracks in Sydney, Australia, another memorial to the Irish Potato Famine, designed by Hossein and Angela Valamanesh (1999), effects a sense of abandonment and pathos. With a table and shelves with the most spare of possessions, a few books, a basket, there is a profoundly melancholy air to the memorial. An empty plate sits on the table. These remainders hold within them small universes of loss. The departure of things, of wholes, of lives, of loves, leaves the pain of residual stains, 'stranded objects'.[107] Inhering within remnants these are the phantom presences that prevent closure, with the paradox that it is *absence* which becomes palpable.

Memorials to individuals too can offer the contemplative experience of melancholy. Those memorials which transcend the object-centred single gesture allow for a sense of slowness and percolation. American landscape architect Lawrence Halprin's memorial to Franklin Delano Roosevelt, on the edge of the Tidal Basin in Washington DC is such a site. It is a memorial which opposes the monolithic and massive gestures of the nearby Lincoln, Washington and Jefferson memorials, and instead is composed of a series of landscape 'rooms', each one a meditation upon phases of Roosevelt's life. Water is a constant present, echoing these phases through its character, and as a whole the memorial seems not about closure, but about experience and engagement. The memorial to Walter Benjamin at Portbou on the border of France and Spain is also an engulfing, experiential site.

This is the place where Benjamin may have committed suicide, while fleeing from Nazi Germany, yet the details of his death remain unclear. Such ambiguity and the resistance to closure are expressed in the memorial designed by Israeli sculptor, Dani Karavan. The memorial, again, is not a simple object, but a serial space which 'little by little, involves your body and soul in meditation and emotion'.[108] Incorporating texts from Benjamin, and based around a connection through a rectangular rusty tunnel, the memorial places the visitor into a relationship with the sea, the sky, and their own shadow projected into the tunnel by the sunlight. The view of the swirling sea below, framed by the rusty tunnel, evokes an image of turmoil, forever in motion, as though possessed by an ongoing energy and agitation.

Ruins

Jean Starobinski writes of ruins in the context of an ancient monument, the very thing that had been established as a 'monition', a perpetuator of memory, and its 'melancholy resides in the fact that it has become a monument of lost significance… but awareness of this oblivion implied awareness of the necessity of remembering.'[109] The role of ruins as a trigger for memory casts them in the role of the *ubi sunt*, the lament of 'where are?', such that contemplating a ruin might bring forth the litany of melancholy loss.

The potency of ruins as repositories for melancholy memories is connected to the paradoxical practice of building ruins. During the eighteenth-century cult of ruins it was common for them to be constructed on English country estates, taking the form of structures like decaying temples. Immediately assuming an air of a past era, they infused the site with the gravity of time passing. The National Monument on Calton Hill in Edinburgh, a memorial to the dead of the Napoleonic Wars, was never finished and thus appears as though a ruin, with its 'melancholy aspect gracing many prints and postcards as if it had been a place of worship for ancient Scots.'[110]

This evocation of the passing of time via ruins is a commentary on the melancholy of our place in time. Louis Kahn designed buildings as ruins to make a nostalgic connection to past ages. 'I thought of the beauty of ruins... of things which nothing lives behind ... and so I thought of wrapping ruins around buildings,' he explained.[111] Controversially, Albert Speer, the architect for the Nazis, developed an idea of 'ruin-value' to anticipate how a building would look once ruined. Through this, he believed, the values that had been instilled into that architecture would persist as some kind of residue within the ruin. He had his Zeppelin stadium at Nuremberg depicted as though in ruin to show how it would look 'after generations of neglect, covered with ivy, with collapsed pillars, the walls here and there fallen down, but in broad outline still clearly recognizable.'[112] British architect John Soane also adopted an idea of ruin-value, of that melancholic yearning for a future that is past, and had Joseph Michael Gandy paint his monumental Bank of England in London (1830) as though it was a ruin. Giambattista Piranesi, the eighteenth-century Italian artist, also sought to evoke a memory for things not yet seen, and the imagery of time claiming structures of grandeur 'command their intensely poignant impact precisely through his interpretation of this melancholic contrast between their past glory and their present dilapidation'.[113]

Thomas Macaulay, the nineteenth-century poet, historian and politician, described a future where a 'New Zealander' (i.e. a Maori), a visitor from an Arcadian paradise, would witness London in ruins. In 1840 he wrote of imagining the melancholy day when 'some traveller from New Zealand shall in the midst of a vast solitude, take his stand on a broken arch of London Bridge to sketch the ruins of St. Paul's.'[114] Gustave Doré made an engraving called *The New Zealander* in 1873, which appears to illustrate Macaulay's vision. The 'wizard-like' figure, the New Zealander in his cloak, holds a sketchbook, and is drawing the ruins of St Paul's.[115] As Woodward suggests, the New Zealander as a visitor from a young colony would have represented the 'dominant civilisation of the future' for Victorians.[116] This vision of seeing London in ruins, as a melancholy spectacle, is the denouement in Bernard Smith's extensive study of *European Vision in the South Pacific*, and as a concluding 'amen' his final words are: '*Et in Arcadia Ego*'.

The prospective envisioning of ruins as objects of latent melancholy is echoed in American environmental artist Robert Smithson's concept of 'ruins in reverse'. Observing the buildings and highways under construction during a field trip to his native suburban Passaic, New Jersey, Smithson wrote, 'That zero panorama seemed to contain *ruins in reverse*, that is – all the new construction that would eventually be built. This is the opposite of the 'romantic ruin' because the buildings don't *fall* into ruin after they are built but rather rise into ruin before they are built.'[117] Passaic becomes, in Smithson's imagining, a place of monuments, a liminal condition, hovering at the crossing over between present and past, solid and void, where space is a form of time. He declares a number of elements of the quotidian suburban landscape as 'monuments', recording them in photographs taken with his Instamatic camera. 'The Fountain Monument', is where six large pipes emerge into the river, and 'The Sand-Box Monument' is a poignant playground terrain, of a wooden box once a container for sand and now simply a type of mark, a ruin. Yet, here it is elevated to a metonymic mnemonic for time immemorial, a small fragment speaking for a much greater memory: 'This monument of minute particles blazed under a bleakly growing sun, and suggested the sullen dissolution of entire continents, the drying up of oceans – no longer were there green forests and high mountains – all that existed were millions of grains of sand, a vast deposit of bones and stones pulverized into dust.'[118]

Drawn to the marginal conditions of suburbia, Smithson's exploration of time within this unheroic landscape sheds light upon the paradox of monuments. Smithson's monuments stand as stranded objects, the very act of his designation removing them from the fabric of the everyday, making them instant, readymade markers of loss. Indeed, Smithson's monuments achieve a melancholy aesthetic through their very imprecision. What, for example, is the Sand-Box Monument (also known as the Desert Monument) a memorial *to*? Smithson describes how it 'became a map of infinite disintegration and forgetfulness', yet it is, perhaps, as much about the enigmatic sense of loss which dogs the melancholic, an indefinable loss of things. If there was a clear sense of what was lost, we could mourn it, grieve it, move on. Yet, this feeling of

objects stranded, branded as monuments, lingering as
wounds, of sadness without a cause, suffuses the suburban
waste-land with eternal poignancy.

These marginal landscapes of loss, the *terrain vague* of
the suburbs and city margins, are significant repositories
of melancholy in the city. The idea of the *terrain vague*
was coined by the Spanish architect and writer, Ignasi de
Solà-Morales Rubió, and based on a phrase from film-
making, meaning an empty, abandoned space.[119] These
were identified as spaces of opportunity within the city,
but unfortunately they are all too often seen as sites of
development. To leave these sites, to allow them to persist as the melancholic ruins for the twenty-first century,
would be a response to the city as self, to the internal
equilibrium required by the city as much as the psyche.
Yet, just as the culture of the pursuit of happiness seeks to
expunge sadness from the human condition, there is a
parallel in the landscape of ruins. Despite, or because of,
the memories that inhere in the decaying industrial hulks,
the abandoned shipyards, the mouldering factories, the
reaction is often to seek to 'tidy' the sites up. This is a
constantly repeated theme, as though the melancholy of
these sites is threatening, inconvenient, antithetical to an
uncomplicated existence. Sites like Sydney's Cockatoo
Island, for example, a former prison and shipbuilding yard,
which was an eerie ruin within the otherwise idyllic harbour. The relics of the prison buildings, the abandoned
cranes and docks, had been left as a slowly decaying site.
Cockatoo Island's dark presence is now being erased, and
the Sydney Harbour Federation Trust is transforming it
into a public park, with places for camping, and interpretation of the remnant elements of the site. This is just one

example of similar projects around the world, where for various reasons – commercial, public safety amidst the industrial ruins, and the suppression of sadness – places of dark memories are replaced by uncomplicated parks.

Darkness and Shadows

The falling of darkness and the play of shadows suggest the time of melancholy. Those liminal times between seasons, and between day and night, evoke the lingering sense of time passing. Darkness can be seen as distinct from light, or from happiness, and both senses are inherent in melancholy. The effect of darkness is profound, as in the description by the psychiatrist Eugène Minkowski: 'Dark space envelops me on all sides and penetrates me much deeper than light space, the distinction between inside and outside and consequently the sense organs as well, insofar as they are designed for external perception, here play only a totally modest role.'[120] Minkowski's description of melting into darkness, of merging with it, is related to the melancholy of camouflage, of disappearing, as Caillois adds, 'While light space is eliminated by the materiality of objects, darkness is "filled", it touches the individual directly, envelops him, penetrates him, and even passes through him: hence "the ego is permeable for darkness while it is not so for light"; the feeling of mystery that one experiences at night would not come from anything else.'[121]

Darkness draws veils, boundaries between things dissolve into the indeterminate light of dusk. The eye succumbs, and there is a drift into poignancy. There is no coincidence that pupil dilation occurs not only with darkness, but also with sadness. An architectural experience of this is the *camera obscura*, literally the 'dark room', but rather than the room used for processing photographs, this is like entering the camera itself. A darkened room with a small hole to the outside world, an aperture, lets in light as a lens does into a camera. This image is projected onto a surface, whether the wall, floor, or a table. The pupil of the eye is dilated in darkness, a physiological occurrence that mimics the state of sadness, and this complements the contemplation inside a *camera obscura*. The outside world is conveyed into the dark space almost like a 'real time' video link, but here it is unmediated by technology; it is real, or more precisely surreal, with its otherworldly quality and praeternatural light. *Camera obscuras* were popular during Victorian and Edwardian times, as a spectacle, and can still be found in places like Foredown Tower, in Portslade, Brighton and the Observatory in Bristol and on the Royal Mile in Edinburgh. A contemporary *camera obscura* was created in the 'Garden of Australian Dreams' at the National Museum of Australia in Canberra, designed by landscape architects, Room 4.1.3 – an echo of darkness of a different kind, as it resembles the helmet of the outlaw Ned Kelly.

Étienne-Louis Boullée, the visionary eighteenth-century French architect, sought the darkness of death in his designs. His 'architecture of shadows' was not so much a play of dark against light, but dark against darker, as he explained, 'the black picture of an architecture of shadows depicted by the effect of even blacker shadows'.[122] This effect had occurred to him when walking in the woods, when he was struck by the sadness in nature, and he wanted to express the extreme melancholy of mourning through the creation of a 'buried architecture'. The ideas are introduced in his *Architecture: Essay on Art*, the subject of melancholy in architecture is explored, and he seeks the means to achieve it. He recalls standing on the edge of the woods in moonlight and suddenly seeing his own shadow:

> By a particular disposition of the mind, the effect of this simulacrum seemed to me to be of an extreme sadness. The trees drawn on the ground by their shadows made the most profound impression on me. This picture grew in my imagination. I then saw everything that was the most somber in nature. What did I see? The mass of objects detached in black against a light of extreme pallor. Nature seemed to offer itself in mourning, to my sight. Struck by the sentiments I felt, I occupied myself, from this moment on, in making its particular application to architecture.[123]

Notes

1. Nick Cave, *The Secret Life of the Love Song; The Flesh made Word*.
2. Jean Clair, 'Saturn's Museum', pp.28 and 32.
3. 2004 Melancholia, LA Freewaves, 9th Biennial Festival of Experimental Media Arts, How Can You Resist? Los Angeles.
4. Seymour Chatman and Paul Duncan, *Michelangelo Antonioni: The Complete Films*, p.95.
5. Ingmar Bergman, *From the Life of the Marionettes*, p.37.
6. Jessie Kalin, *The Films of Ingmar Bergman*, p.131.
7. Ingmar Bergman, *The Seventh Seal: A Film*, p.39.
8. Andrei Tarkovsky in Vida T Johnson, and Graham Petrie, *The Films of Andrei Tarkovsky: A Visual Fugue*, p.159.
9. Raymond Klibansky, Erwin Panofsky and Fritz Saxl, *Saturn and Melancholy: Studies in the History of Natural Philosophy, Religion and Art*, p.323.
10. Roland Barthes, *Camera Lucida*, p.79.

11. Chris Marker, *Immemory*.

12. Walter Benjamin, 'The Work of Art in the Age of Mechanical Reproduction', p.226.

13. Hubert Damisch, 'Five Notes for a Phenomenology of the Photographic Image', p.72.

14. John Dixon Hunt in Pia Maria Simig, *Fleur de L'Air: A Garden in Provence by Ian Hamilton Finlay*, no page numbers.

15. See Marco de Michelis and Robert Fitzpatrick, *Hiroshi Sugimoto: Architecture*.

16. Giovanni Chiaramonte and Andrey A Tarkovsky, *Instant Light: Tarkovsky Polaroids*.

17. Tonino Guerra in ibid, p.9.

18. *Sunday Star Times Magazine*, 29 January 2006, p.17.

19. Allan Smith, 'Romanticist and Symbolist Tendencies in Recent New Zealand Photography', p.111.

20. Robert Leonard cited in Justin Paton, 'Living Proof'. In Laurence Aberhart, *Aberhart*, p.282.

21. Walter Benjamin, 'The Work of Art in the Age of Mechanical Reproduction', p.222-223.

22. Justin Paton, 'Living Proof'. In Laurence Aberhart, *Aberhart*, p.280.

23. Charles W. Haxthausen, 'Review: Gerhard Richter. New York'.

24. Octavio Paz, 'Objects and Apparitions – for Joseph Cornell' (trans. Elizabeth Bishop). In Dore Ashton, *A Cornell Album*, p.115.

25. *Vanitas* means 'emptiness' in Latin, a reference to life's transience. *Vanitas* painting was developed in the Netherlands and Flanders in the sixteenth and seventeenth centuries, and was a technique of still life painting, in which the objects depicted were imbued with particular symbolic dimensions. These items were *memento mori* – reminders of death – like skulls, fading flowers, rotting fruit, and symbols of time such as hourglasses and clocks.

26. Rachel Carley, 'Domestic Afterlives: Rachel Whiteread's *Ghost*', p.26.

27. See, for example, Iain Sinclair, *London: City of Disappearances*.

28. Rachel Lichtenstein in Rachel Lichtenstein and Iain Sinclair, *Rodinsky's Room*, p.32.

29. See for example Herve Chandes, *Francesca Woodman*.

30. Jordan Cantor, 'Tacita Dean at Peter Blum Gallery 2002', p.138.

31. EM Cioran, *On the Heights of Despair*, p.30.

32. Anselm Kiefer in Alan Riding, 'An Artist sets up House(s) at the Grand Palais'.

33. Bernd Heinrich Wilhelm von Kleist cited in Linda Siegel, 'Synaesthesia and the Paintings of Caspar David Friedrich', p.204.

34. See Peter Toohey and Kathleen Toohey (2004), 'Giorgio de Chirico, Time, Odysseus, Melancholy, and Intestinal Disorder'.

35. Olaf Blanke Theodor Landis, 'The Metaphysical Art of Giorgio de Chirico: Migraine or Epilepsy?'.

36. Rolf Günter Renner, *Edward Hopper, 1882-1967: Transformation of the Real*, p.80.

37. See Susanne Lange, *Bernd and Hilla Becher: Life and Work*.

38. See Constance Glenn, Virginia Heckert and Mary-Jane Lombino, *Candida Höfer: The Architecture of Absence*.

39. See Peter Galassi, *Andreas Gursky*. New York: Abrams.

40. See Thomas Ruff and Matthias Winzen, *Thomas Ruff: Photography 1979 to the Present*.

41. Guy Tosatto, 'The Time of Photography'. In Thomas Struth, *Still*, p.12.

42. Carol Diehl, 'The Toxic Sublime', p.120.

43. See Edward Burtynsky and Lori Pauli, *Manufactured Landscapes: The Photographs of Edward Burtynsky*.

44. See for example the new translation in the Modern Library series, Johann Wolfgang Von Goethe, *The Sorrows of Young Werther*.

45. François-René Chateaubriand, *Atala and René*.

46. Aleksandr Sergeevich Pushkin, *Eugene Onegin*.

47. James Beattie, *The Poetical Works of James Beattie*, p.129.

48. David Fairer, Christine Gerrard, *Eighteenth-century Poetry: An Annotated Anthology*, p.392.

49. André Breton, *Nadja*, pp.159-160.

50. WG Sebald, *The Rings of Saturn*, p.11.

51. ibid, pp.63-65.

52. WG Sebald, *The Emigrants*.

53. WG Sebald, *Vertigo*.

54. Sigmund Freud, *Civilization and Its Discontents*, pp.17–18.

55. Orhan Pamuk, *Istanbul: Memories of a City*, p.80.

56. ibid, p.95

57. Georges Rodenbach, *Bruges-la-Morte*, p.73.

58. ibid, p.72.

59. Gustave Flaubert, *November*, p.21.

60. Joris-Karl Huysmans, *Against Nature*, p.133.

61. Gustave Flaubert, *November,* p.90.

62. ibid, p.24–25.

63. Roger Caillois, 'Mimicry and Legendary Psychasthenia', p.20.

64. Joris-Karl Huysmans, *Against Nature*, p.133.

65. Georges Rodenbach, *Bruges-la-Morte*, p.21.

66. Alastair Hannay, 'Introduction' in Søren Kierkegaard, *Either/Or: A Fragment of Life*, p.9.

67. Gustave Flaubert, *November*, p.21.

68. WG Sebald, *Vertigo*, p.35.

69. Jean-Paul Sartre, *Nausea*, p.43.

70. WG Sebald, *The Rings of Saturn*, p.205.

71. From the *Dictionary of Received Ideas* in Gustave Flaubert, *Bouvard and Pécuchet*, p.316.

72. Orhan Pamuk, *Istanbul: Memories of a City*, p.141.

73. Italo Calvino, *If on a Winter's Night a Traveller*, p.258.

74. Robert Burton, *An Anatomy of Melancholy*, p.459–460.

75. Raymond Klibansky, Erwin Panofsky and Fritz Saxl, *Saturn and Melancholy: Studies in the History of Natural Philosophy, Religion and Art*, p.231.

76. Jon Pareles, 'Melancholy Melodies in Armenian Tradition'.

77. Edward Bunting, *The Ancient Music of Ireland*, p.58.

78. Federico García Lorca, *In Search of Duende*, p.49.

79. Cited in Shelia Fitzpatrick, 'Happiness and *Toska*: An Essay in the History of Emotions in Pre-war Soviet Russia', p.368.

80. Raymond Klibansky, Erwin Panofsky and Fritz Saxl, *Saturn and Melancholy: Studies in the History of Natural Philosophy, Religion and Art*, pp.238–239, note 59.

81. W Wright Roberts, 'The Problem of Satie', p.315.

82. Geoff Smith, 'An Interview with Arvo Pärt: Sources of Invention', p.24.

83. Wilfrid Howard Mellers, *Celestial Music?: Some Masterpieces of European Religious Music*, p.14.

84. Ivan Moody, 'Giya Kancheli: An Introduction to His Music', p.50.

85. Victor Shklovlsky, 'Art as Technique'.

86. Susan Bradshaw, 'Giya Kancheli – 'Life without Christmas".

87. Christopher Mark, 'Messiaen: 'Quatuor pour la fin du temps' by Anthony Pople', p.144.

88. Michael Gordon, Sleeve notes, *Decasia: The State of Decay*.

89. Geoffrey Himes, 'Tom Waits', In Mark Montandon, *Innocent When You Dream: The Tom Waits Reader*, p.57.

90. Tom Waits, *Nighthawks at the Diner*.

91. Tom Waits, *Alice*.

92. Nick Cave, *Murder Ballads*.

93. Robert Burton, *An Anatomy of Melancholy*, p.xi.

94. Nick Cave, *Abattoir Blues*.

95. Nick Cave, *The Secret Life of the Love Song; The Flesh made Word*. Also in Nick Cave, *The Complete Lyrics 1978-2001*.

96. Nick Cave, *No More Shall We Part*.

97. Nick Cave, *The Secret Life of the Love Song; The Flesh made Word*. Also in Nick Cave, *The Complete Lyrics 1978-2001*.

98. Nick Cave, *The Boatman's Call*.

99. ibid.

100. Alain de Botton, *The Architecture of Happiness*.

101. Thomas Moore, *The Care of the Soul*, p.46.

102. Susan Sontag, *Illness as Metaphor and AIDS and its Metaphors*, p.50.

103. Orhan Pamuk *Istanbul: Memories of a City*, frontispiece.

104. Roy Strong, *The Renaissance Garden in England*, p.216.

105. Rico Franses, 'Monuments and Melancholia'.

106. In Jacky Bowring, 'To Make the Stone[s] Stony: Defamiliarization and Andy Goldsworthy's Garden of Stones', p.184.

107. 'Stranded objects' is Eric Santner's term, who in turn attributes it to a colleague who provided it unknowingly. See Eric L Santner, *Stranded Objects: Mourning, Memory and Film in Postwar Germany*.

108. Germain Viatte, 'Passages', In *Dani Karavan: Passages – Homage to Walter Benjamin*, p.78.

109. Jean Starobinski, *The Invention of Liberty, 1700-1789*, p.180.

110. Susan Stewart, 'Garden Agon', p.119.

111. See Kent Larson, *Louis I. Kahn: Unbuilt Masterworks*.

112. In Jürgen Straub, *Narration, Identity and Historical Consciousness*, p.249.

113. Tarnya Cooper, 'Forgetting Room and the voice of Piranesi's 'Speaking Ruins'', p.115.

114. Thomas Macaulay in Bernard H Smith, *European Vision and the South Pacific*, p.332.

115. See Gustave Doré and Blanchard Jerrold, *London: A Pilgrimage*.

116. Christopher Woodward, *In Ruins*, p.1.

117. Robert Smithson in Ann Reynolds, *Robert Smithson: Learning from New Jersey and Elsewhere*, p.114.

118. Robert Smithson, 'The Monuments of Passaic', p.51.

119. Ignasi de Solà-Morales Rubió, 'Terrain Vague'. In Cynthia Davidson (ed) *Anyplace*.

120. In Roger Caillois, 'Mimicry and Legendary Psychasthenia', p.30.

121. ibid.

122. Boullée in Anthony Vidler, *The Architectural Uncanny: Essays in the Modern Unhomely*, p.170.

123. Boullée in ibid, pp.168–170.

By Way of Conclusion:
Melancholy and the Imagination

6

By Way of Conclusion: Melancholy and the Imagination

There is no imagination that is not overtly, or secretly, melancholy.
Julia Kristeva, *Black Sun*[1]

The *Field Guide* began by announcing its advocacy of melancholy, and ends with the entreaty that while an 'architecture of happiness' is necessary, so too is an architecture of sadness, all of those words and worlds where melancholy can inhere, a habitat for a depth of being.

The complexities and contradictions of melancholy's place within the science of psychiatry, and the aspiration towards a 'cure', will continue to be in tension with melancholy's association with genius, beauty, and creative impetus. The worry is that the over-diagnosis of melancholia, and the treatment of sadness, will throw the baby out with the bathwater. To lose the depths of melancholic contemplation as a consequence of the elimination of sadness is a spectre which haunts the objectification of melancholy.

David Cooper, in his introduction to Michel Foucault's seminal work *Madness and Civilization,* described how in reading the book:

one is awakened to a tragic sense of the loss involved in the relegation of the wildly charismatic or inspirational area of our experience to the desperate region of pseudo-medical categorization from which clinical psychiatry has sprung. [2]

This profoundly resonates with another potent passage from that same year, Giorgio Agamben's lament for the relegation of the imagination in contemporary culture:

> Nothing can convey the extent of the change that has taken place in the meaning of experience so much as the resulting reversal of the status of the imagination. For Antiquity, the imagination, which is now expunged from knowledge as 'unreal,' was the supreme medium of knowledge. [3]

To lose melancholy is to be deprived of one of the imagination's refuges, the dark interior realm where thoughts fly. They fuel one another. Melancholy slows things, allows for percolation, facilitates solitude and solace for imagination. And imagination makes space for melancholy, they work together to construct the allied experiences of nostalgia, reverie, sorrow, shadows. The *Field Guide* proffers destinations for the imagination, an aerial perspective, an overview, a tool for embracing the human condition.

Notes
1. Julia Kristeva, *Black Sun: Depression and Melancholia*, p.6.
2. David Cooper, Introduction. In Michel Foucault, *Madness and Civilization: A History of Insanity in the Age of Reason*, p.viii.
3. Giorgio Agamben, *Infancy and History: On the Destruction of Experience*, p.11.

A Note on Laurence Aberhart

7

A Note on Laurence Aberhart

Laurence Aberhart's photographs are 'eloquent ciphers for loss, time and beauty'.[1] In their curious emptiness, stillness, they evoke the very core of a melancholy which seems both universal, and also particularly tuned to the darkness of New Zealand. When contemplating the question, 'What does melancholy look like?', Aberhart's photographs would come to mind, their brooding presence recalling memories that remain mired somewhere just beyond the present. The images in this book capture just a small fragment of his oeuvre, many of which featured in a major show which has toured New Zealand over the past couple of years, and which is represented by the book *Aberhart*.[2] The cover image of the *Field Guide*, 'Last Light, Tolaga Bay, 30 May 1989', presents an icon of melancholy; hovering at a liminal place, where the sea meets the sky, at a liminal time, the time of twilight. And it is, as in the case of the most profoundly melancholy events, a paradox. Tolaga Bay is located on New Zealand's East Coast, and it is the part of the country, and the world, that sees the first light of every day, such is its proximity to the dateline, and it is here that Aberhart captures the 'last light'. The keying into time, that singular preoccupation of melancholy, of Saturn, of Chronos, is carefully marked in Aberhart's work. Across the four decades of his oeuvre, each photograph has its exact date as part of the title.

Laurence Aberhart's work is represented in all of the major galleries in New Zealand, as well as in Australia at the National Gallery of Australia, Canberra; Museum of Contemporary Art, Sydney; and Queensland Art Gallery, Brisbane. In the USA his work is in the Readers Digest Collection, Pleasantville, and the Hallmark Card Collection, Kansas City. And in France at the Bibliotheque Nationale, Paris. Aberhart has been awarded Fulbright and Moet and Chandon Fellowships, and has been the artist in residence at the Dunedin Public Art Gallery. Recent exhibitions include *Serial Works: Last Light & Domestic Architecture*, Darren Knight Gallery, Sydney, Australia (2003); *Laurence Aberhart*, The Stedelijk Museum of Modern Art, Amsterdam, The Netherlands (2002); *Asia*, Darren Knight Gallery, Sydney, Australia; *Macau, China, Japan*, Sue Crockford Gallery, Auckland, New Zealand; *Ghostwriting: Photographs of Macau*, Macau Museum of Art, Macau; John Batten Gallery, Hong Kong; *Laurence Aberhart in Japan*, Dunedin Public Art Gallery, New Zealand (2001).

Acknowledgements

Thanks to Darren Knight Gallery, Sydney, Australia, for supplying the cover image, and to Victoria University Press, Wellington, New Zealand, for the remaining images. Special thanks to Laurence Aberhart for the use of his photographs.

Notes
1. David Eggleton, *Into the Light: A History of New Zealand Photography*, p.146.
2. Laurence Aberhart, *Aberhart*.

Further Reading and Bibliography

Melancholy, melancholia, and all that circles around it, is a vast sphere of thought. While this *Field Guide* is intended as a means of appreciating the idea of melancholy, by necessity it can only hint at some of the extensive debates and discourses on the topic. There are some substantial major works on melancholy, with particular thematic or disciplinary focuses. In terms of melancholy within art, Klibansky, Panofsky and Saxl's significant tome on *Saturn and Melancholy* traces that particular thread in great detail, with the culmination of the work being a thorough discussion of Dürer's *Melencolia I.* A critique of Klibansky, Panofsky and Saxl's discussion is developed by Giorgio Agamben in *Stanzas* (1993). More recently, a major exhibition on melancholy in art was staged by the Galeries Nationales du Grand Palais in Paris (2005), and the catalogue, *Mélancolie: Génie et Folie en Occident,* published by Gallimard is a comprehensive overview of the various melancholic expressions in art. It is well-illustrated, and contains essays on a number of themes. To date, the catalogue is only available in French.

A number of the historic texts on melancholy have been republished and are available as recent editions. There is a range of versions of Robert Burton's *Anatomy of Melancholy*, including the very accessible short version published by Dover, *The Essential Anatomy of Melancholy*

(2002). Unfortunately Klibansky, Panofsky and Saxl's key work, *Saturn and Melancholy* has never been republished, and the only editions are those from 1964. Some foreign-language editions are available through specialist rare bookshops, but copies in English seem even rarer. Andrés Velázquez's *Libro de la Melancholia* (1585) was recently republished by M. Baroni (2002), but is only available in Spanish. Jacques Ferrand's *A Treatise on Lovesickness* (1623) was translated into English and published by Syracuse University Press (1994).

Jennifer Radden's *The Nature of Melancholy: From Aristotle to Kristeva* (2000) presents a number of extracts from key sources, and a major critical essay, with an emphasis on the history of psychology. A complementary source to this is the earlier work by Stanley W Jackson, *Melancholia and Depression: From Hippocratic Times to Modern Times* (1986), which presents a chronology of the relationship between melancholia and clinical depression. And even earlier, Michel Foucault's seminal *Madness and Civilization: A History of Insanity in the Age of Reason* (1961) is useful further reading for a deconstruction of 'mental illness' including melancholia.

Two recent conferences present a breadth of scholarship on melancholy. From the realm of the humanities, 'Culture and Melancholy' was the topic of the conference held in 2002 at the University of Kent, England, with papers published in *Journal of European Studies,* Vol. 33, 2003. As is characteristic of many studies of melancholy, the conference exhibited melancholy's resistance to a simple explanation. And from the domain of science, the conference 'Melancholia: Beyond DSM, Beyond Neurotransmitters' was held in Copenhagen, Denmark in 2006, with papers published in a special issue 433 of *Acta Psychiatrica Scandinavica*, 2007. Again the discourse is characterised by a grappling for definitions of melancholia.

There are also a number of more specific studies, exploring melancholy at particular time periods or tight disciplinary focuses, for example Jeremy Schmidt's *Melancholy and the Care of the Soul* which focuses on Early Modern England and Max Penksy's *Melancholy Dialectics: Walter Benjamin and the Play of Mourning* which provides a detailed overview of the early twentieth century as it relates to Benjamin and his peers. The melancholy of the twentieth century in relation to issues of race is explored in Paul Gilroy's *Postcolonial Melancholia* and Anne Anlin Cheng's *The Melancholy of Race*. Dylan Trigg's book on *The Aesthetics of Decay* and Robert Ginsburg's on *The Aesthetics of Ruins* explore some of the haunts of melancholy, and provide useful complementary reading.

In the field of psychology, and particularly psychoanalysis, Julia Kristeva's *Black Sun* is an important source on the relationship of melancholy to the human condition. The writings of Hannah Segal and Melanie Klein both extend the work on Freudian psychoanalysis and melancholy, developing their own ideas, for example in the relationships to the death drive, and to the creative impulse. Esther Sanchez-Pardos's *Cultures of the Death Drive: Melanie Klein and Modernist Melancholia* provides an in-depth discussion, and relates Klein's works to the reading of contemporary literature. For further reading on the specific relationship between melancholy and genius see Kay Redfield Jamison's *Touched with Fire: Manic-Depressive Illness and the Artistic Temperament*. Further reading in the area of psychiatry covers a vast spectrum ranging from

Peter D Kramer's promotion of the psychiatric perspective on melancholy as depression to Dan G Blazer's *The Age of Melancholy* which supports the efforts psychiatry needs to make, not only in pharmaceutical terms, but also in reaching a better understanding of the sociology of depression. Blazer voices concerns over the numbing effects of contemporary culture, longer working hours, increasing individualisation and isolation, and assaults by the advertising industry. At the other extreme, Allan V Horwitz and Jerome C Wakefield's *The Loss of Sadness*, takes the view that psychiatry is constructing illness for diagnosis, and this is causing a substantial exaggeration in the terrain of mental illness. Eric G Wilson's *Against Happiness: In Praise of Melancholy* argues for melancholia as an essential part of creativity.

Memoirs of melancholia, or what are more recently called 'depression memoirs' are a further form of reading on melancholia. In *Speaking of Sadness: Depression, Disconnection, and the Meanings of Illness* David Carp recounts his own, and his interviewees' experience of depression. Rick Moody's *The Black Veil* is one of the most well-known of such contemporary accounts.

Bibliography

2004 Melancholia, LA Freewaves, 9th Biennial Festival of Experimental Media Arts, How Can You Resist? Los Angeles

Aberhart, Laurence, *Aberhart*, Wellington: Victoria University Press, 2007

Ackroyd, Peter, *Hawksmoor*, London: Abacus, 1986

Adorno, Theodor, *Kierkegaard: Construction of the Aesthetic* (trans. Robert Hullot-Kentor), Minneapolis: University of Minnesota

Press, 1989

Agamben, Giorgio, *Stanzas: Word and Phantasm in Western Culture* (Theory and History of Literature, volume 69) (trans. Ronald L Martinez), Minneapolis: University of Minnesota Press, 1993

Agamben, Giorgio, *Infancy and History: On the Destruction of Experience* (trans. Liz Heron), London: Verso, 2007. (Originally published in 1978 as *Infanza e storia*)

Akiskal, Hagop S and Kareen K Akiskal, 'In search of Aristotle: Temperament, human nature, melancholia, creativity and eminence', *Journal of Affective Disorders*, 100: 1–6. 2007

Akiskal, Hagop S and Kareen K Akiskal, 'A mixed state core for melancholia: an exploration in history, art and clinical science', *Acta Psychiatrica Scandinavica,* 115 (supplement 433): 44–49. 2007

Aronson, Jeffrey K and Manoj Ramachandran, 'The diagnosis of art: melancholy and the Portrait of Dr Gachet', *Journal of the Royal Society of Medicine,* 99: 373–374. 2006

Ashton, Dore, *A Cornell Album*, New York: Da Capo Press, 1989

Bachelard, Gaston, *The Poetics of Reverie*, Boston: Beacon Press, 1971

Bachelard, Gaston, *The Poetics of Space* (trans. Maria Jolas), Boston: Beacon, 1994. (First published 1958 as *La poétique d'espace*)

Barthes, Roland, *Camera Lucida*, London: Fontana, 1984 (Originally published 1980)

Baudelaire, Charles, *Intimate Journals* (trans. Don Bachardy), London: Black Spring Press, 1989. (First published 1930)

Baudelaire, Charles, *Paris Spleen* (trans. Louise Varèse), New York: New Directions Books, 1970. (First published 1869)

Baudelaire, Charles, *The Flowers of Evil*, (trans. William Aggeler), Fresno, CA: Academy Library Guild, 1954

Beattie, James, *The Poetical Works of James Beattie* Manchester, NH: Ayer Publishing, 1972 (first published 1831)

Benjamin, Walter, 'The Work of Art in the Age of Mechanical Reproduction' in *Illuminations* (trans Harry Zohn), New York: Schocken Books, 1968

Bergman, Ingmar, *From the Life of the Marionettes* (trans. Alan Blair), New York: Pantheon, 1980

Bergman, Ingmar, *The Seventh Seal: A Film,* New York: Simon and Schuster, 1960

Blazer, Dan G, *The Age of Melancholy: 'Major Depression' and its Social Origins,* New York: Routledge, 2005

Blunt, Anthony, 'Reviewed work(s): Poussin's Et in Arcadia Ego'. *The Art Bulletin,* 20(1): 96–100. 1938

Botton, Alain de, *The Architecture of Happiness,* London: Penguin Books, 2006

Bowring, Jacky, 'To Make the Stone[s] Stony: Defamiliarization and Andy Goldsworthy's Garden of Stones', In Michel Conan (ed). *Contemporary Garden Aesthetics, Creations, and Interpretations,* Washington, DC: Dumbarton Oaks, 2007

Boym, Svetlana, *The Future of Nostalgia,* New York: Basic Books, 2001

Bradshaw, Susan, 'Giya Kancheli – 'Life without Christmas'', *Tempo,* New Series, No. 196: 47. 1996

Braun, Wilhelm Alfred, *Types of Weltschmerz in German Poetry,* New York: Columbia University Press, 1905

Breton, André, *Nadja.* (trans. Richard Howard). London: Penguin Books, 1999 (First published 1928)

Bronfen, Elisabeth, *Over Her Dead Body: Death, Femininity and the Aesthetic,* Manchester: Manchester University Press, 1992

Brown, Wendy, 'Resisting Left Melancholy', *Boundary 2,* 26(3)19-27. 1999

Bunting, Edward, *The Ancient Music of Ireland,* New York: Dover, 2000. (Originally published in 3 volumes, 1773–1843)

Burton, Robert, *An Anatomy of Melancholy,* London: J Cuthell, 1821. (First published 1621)

Burtynsky, Edward and Lori Pauli, *Manufactured Landscapes: The Photographs of Edward Burtynsky,* New Haven: Yale University Press, 2003

Caillois, Roger, 'Mimicry and Legendary Psychasthenia' (trans. John Shepley) (Original essay published 1935). *October,* 31:16-32. 1984

Calvino, Italo, *If on a Winter's Night a Traveller,* (trans. William Weaver), Toronto: Lester and Orpen Dennys, 1981

Calvino, Italo, *Six Memos for the New Millennium,* Cambridge, MA: Harvard University Press, 1988

Campbell, Joseph, *Sukhavati,* (DVD) Acacia, 1998

Camus, Albert, *The Myth of Sisyphus,* New York: Vintage, 1991

Cantor, Jordan. 'Tacita Dean at Peter Blum Gallery 2002', *Artforum*

International 40(7) (March 2002): 138

Carley, Rachel, 'Domestic Afterlives: Rachel Whiteread's *Ghost'*, *Architectural Design*, 78(3): 26-29, p.26. 2008

Carrick, EF, *A Calendar of British Taste from 1600 to 1800*, London: Routledge and Kegan Paul Ltd, 1949

Casey, Edward, *Remembering: A Phenomenological Study*, Bloomington: Indiana University Press, 2000

Cave, Nick. *Abattoir Blues*, a two album boxed set together with *The Lyre of Orpheus*, Mute Records, 2004

Cave, Nick, *The Boatman's Call*, Mute Records, 1997

Cave, Nick, *The Complete Lyrics 1978-2001*, London: Penguin Books, 2001

Cave, Nick, *Murder Ballads*, Mute Records, 1996

Cave, Nick, *No More Shall We Part*, Mute Records, 2001

Cave, Nick, *The Secret Life of the Love Song; The Flesh made Word*, (sound recording), London: King Mob, 2000

Chandes, Herve (ed), *Francesca Woodman*, Zurich: Scalo, 1998

Chateaubriand, François-René. *Atala and René* (trans. Rayner Heppenstall), London: Oxford University Press, 1963. (First published as two separate volumes, *Atala* in 1801 and *René* in 1802)

Chatman, Seymour and Paul Duncan, *Michelangelo Antonioni: The Complete Films*, Köln: Taschen, 2004

Chiaramonte, Giovanni and Andrey A Tarkovsky, *Instant Light: Tarkovsky Polaroids*, London: Thames and Hudson, 2004

Chirico, Giorgio de, *The Memoires of Giorgio de Chirico*, New York: Da Capo Press, 1994

Cioran, EM, *All Gall is Divided* (trans. Richard Howard), New York: Arcade Publishing, 1999. (First published in French 1952)

Cioran, EM, *On the Heights of Despair* (trans. Ilinca Zarifopol-Johnston), Chicago: University of Chicago Press, 1992. (First published in Romanian in 1934)

Cioran, EM, *Tears and Saints* (trans. Ilinca Zarifopol-Johnston), Chicago: University of Chicago Press, 1995. (First published in Romanian, 1937)

Clair, Jean, 'Saturn's Museum', *FMR*, April/May 2005: 27-54. 2005

Clark, David L, 'Heidegger's Craving: Being-on-Schelling', *Diacritics*, 27(3): 8-33. 1997

Clark, Hugh, 'Sakutorō and the City', *Japanese Studies,* 23(2):141-155. 2003

Cook, ET and Alexander Wedderburn (eds), *The Works of John Ruskin,* Volume VI, London: George Allen, 1904

Cooper, David, 'Introduction'. In Michel Foucault, *Madness and Civilization: A History of Insanity in the Age of Reason* (trans. Richard Howard), London: Routledge, 1971. (Originally published 1961 as *Histoire de la Folie*)

Cooper, Tarnya, 'Forgetting Room and the voice of Piranesi's "Speaking Ruins" in Adrian Forty and Süsanne Kuchler (eds) *The Art of Forgetting,* Oxford: Berg, 2001

Damisch, Hubert, 'Five Notes for a Phenomenology of the Photographic Image', *October,* Vol. 5, Summer: 70-72. 1978

Dean, Tacita, *Tacita Dean,* Barcelona: Museu d'Art Contemporani de Barcelona, 2000

Dickens, Charles, *The Chimes,* in the anthology *Christmas Books,* London: Oxford University Press, 1954. (*The Chimes* first published 1844)

Diehl, Carol, 'The Toxic Sublime', *Art in America,* 94(2): 118-124. 2006

Dolan, Elizabeth A, 'British Romantic melancholia: Charlotte Smith's *Elegiac Sonnets,* medical discourse and the problem of sensibility', *Journal of European Studies* 33(3/4): 237-253. 2003

Doré, Gustave and Blanchard Jerrold, *London: A Pilgrimage.* London: Harper and Brothers, 1890

Doughty, Oswald, 'The English Malady of the Eighteenth Century', *The Review of English Studies,* 2(7):257-269. 1925

Eco, Umberto, *Art and Beauty in the Middle Ages,* New Haven: Yale University Press, 1986.

Eco, Umberto (ed). *History of Beauty* (2nd edition), New York: Rizzoli, 2005.

Eco, Umberto (ed) *On Ugliness,* New York: Rizzoli, 2007

Edmond, Martin, 'The Abandoned House as a Refuge for the Imagination', In *Waimarino County & other excursions.* Auckland: Auckland University Press, 2007

Eggleton, David, *Into the Light: A History of New Zealand Photography,* Nelson, NZ: Craig Potton Publishing, 2006

Erdman, David V (ed) *The Complete Poetry and Prose of William Blake,*

Berkeley: University of California Press, 1997

Fairer, David and Christine Gerrard, *Eighteenth-century Poetry: An Annotated Anthology*, Oxford: Blackwell Publishing, 2004

Ferguson, Harvie, *Melancholy and the Critique of Modernity: Søren Kierkegaard's Religious Psychology*, London: Routledge, 1995

Fink, M and Taylor MA, 'Resurrecting melancholia', *Acta Psychiatrica Scandinavica*, 115, special issue 433 Melancholia: Beyond DSM, Beyond Neurotransmitters: 14–20. 2007

Fitzpatrick, Shelia, 'Happiness and *Toska*: An Essay in the History of Emotions in Pre-war Soviet Russia', *Australian Journal of Politics and History,* 50(3): 357–371. 2004

Flaubert, Gustave, *Dictionary of Received Ideas* in *Bouvard and Pécuchet* (trans. AJ Krailsheimer), London: Penguin, 1976

Flaubert, Gustave, *November* (trans. Andrew Brown), London: Hesperus Press Limited, 2005. (First published as *Novembre* in *Oeuvre de jeunesse*, 1910).

Franses, Rico, 'Monuments and Melancholia', *Journal of the Psychoanalysis of Culture and Society,* 6(1): 97–104. 2001

Freud, Sigmund, *Civilization and Its Discontents*, London: Hogarth Press, 1946. (First published 1929)

Freud, Sigmund, *On Murder, Mourning and Melancholia* (trans. Shaun Whiteside), London: Penguin Books, 2005. (Mourning and Melancholia essay first published 1917)

Fritsch, Ingrid, '*Chindonya* Today: Japanese Street Performers in Commercial Advertising', *Asian Folklore Studies, 60:* 49–78. 2001

Galassi, Peter, *Andreas Gursky,* New York: Abrams, 2001

Gallop, Rodney, 'The Fado (The Portuguese Song of Fate)', *The Musical Quarterly,* 19(2): 199–213. 1933

Gellius, Aulus, *Attic Nights* (trans. William Beloe), London: J. Johnson, 1795

Ginsburg, Robert, *The Aesthetics of Ruins*, Amsterdam: Rodopi, 2004

Ginzburg, Natalia, *The Little Virtues* (trans. Dick Davis), New York: Arcade Publishing, 1989

Glenn, Constance, Virginia Heckert and Mary-Jane Lombino, *Candida Höfer: The Architecture of Absence*, New York: Aperture, 2005

Goethe, Johann Wolfgang von, *The Sorrows of Young Werther* (trans. RD Boylan), New York: Mondial, 2006. (First published 1774)

Good, John Mason, Olinthus Gregory and Newton Bosworth, *Pantologia: A New Cabinet Cyclopaedia, Comprehending a Complete Series of Essays, Treatises and Systems, Alphabetically Arranged, with a General Dictionary of Arts, Sciences, and Words*, 12 vols. London: J. Walker, 1819

Gordon, Michael, Sleeve notes, *Decasia: The State of Decay*, DVD, New York: Pexifilm, 2004

Graaf, John de, David Wann and Thomas H. Naylor, *Affluenza: The All-Consuming Epidemic*, San Francisco: Berrett-Koehler, 2002

Hamilton, Clive and Richard Denniss, *Affluenza: when too much is never enough,* Sydney: Allen & Unwin, 2005

Hannay, Alastair, Introduction in Søren Kierkegaard, *Either/Or: A Fragment of Life* (trans. Alastair Hannay), London: Penguin, 1992. (First published 1843)

Harkins, Jean and Anna Wierzbicka (eds), *Emotions in crosslinguistic perspective*, Berlin: Mouton de Gruyter, 2001

Haxthausen, Charles W, 'Review: Gerhard Richter. New York', *The Burlington Magazine,* 138(1114): 56-57. 1996

Herzog, Werner, *Where the Green Ants Dream*. DVD, Xenon Entertainment, 1984

Himes, Geoffrey, 'Tom Waits' in Mark Montandon *Innocent When You Dream: The Tom Waits Reader*, New York: Thunder's Mouth Press, 2005

Hoff, Anton J van, *From Autothanasia to Suicide: Self-Killing in Classical Antiquity*, London: Routledge, 1990

Honkonen, Vesa, 'A letter for Steven Holl to explain the behaviour of Finnish people', available on the architect's website: http://www.vesahonkonenarchitects.com/

Horwitz, Allan V and Jerome C Wakefield, *The Loss of Sadness: How Psychiatry transformed Normal Sorrow into Depressive Disorder*, Oxford: Oxford University Press, 2007

Houaiss, Antonio, *Dicionario Houaiss da lingua portuguesa*, Rio de Janeiro: Objetiva, 2001

Hugo, Victor, *Toilers of the Sea* (trans. W Moy Thomas), London: Sampson Low, Son, and Marston, 1866

Hunt, John Dixon in Pia Maria Simig (ed), *Fleur de L'Air: A Garden in Provence by Ian Hamilton Finlay*, Lanark, Scotland: Wild Hawthorn Press, 2004

Hunt, Leigh, *A Book for a Corner, Or, Selections in Prose and Verse from Authors*, New York: Putnam, 1852

Huysmans, Joris-Karl, *Against Nature* (trans. Robert Baldick), London: Penguin Books, 2003. (First published as *A Rebours*, which is sometimes translated as 'Against the Grain', in 1884)

Isokangas, Antti , 'Finnish Tango: Once a Fad, the Dance is now a Tradition', *Billboard,* February 12 1994, p1 and 78

Jackson, Stanley W, *Melancholia and Depression: From Hippocratic Times to Modern Times*, New Haven: Yale University Press, 1986

Jadhav, Sushrut, 'The Cultural Origins of Western Depression', *The International Journal of Psychiatry*, 42(4): 269-286. 1996

Jamison, Kay Redfield, *Touched with Fire: Manic-Depressive Illness and the Artistic Temperament,* New York, The Free Press, 1993

Jimenez, Mary Ann, 'Madness in Early American History: Insanity in Massachusetts from 1700-1830', *Journal of Social History,* 20(1): 25-44. 1986

Johnson, Samuel, *A Dictionary of the English Language*, London: William Pickering, 1828 (First published 1755)

Johnson, Vida T, and Graham Petrie, *The Films of Andrei Tarkovsky: A Visual Fugue*, Bloomington: Indiana University Press, 1994

Jonson, Ben, *Five Plays*, Oxford: Oxford University Press, 1999 (First published 1598)

Juniper, Andrew, *Wabi-Sabi: The Japanese Art of Impermanence,* Boston: Tuttle Publishing, 2003

Kakuichi, *The Tale of the Heiki* (trans. Helen Craig McCullough), Palo Alto, CA: Stanford University Press, 1988

Kalin, Jessie, *The Films of Ingmar Bergman*, Cambridge: Cambridge University Press, 2003

Kant, Immanuel, *The Critique of Judgment,* (trans. James Creed Meredith), Oxford: Oxford University Press, 1911 (First published in German in 1790)

Kant, Immanuel, *The Critique of Judgment* (trans. JH Bernard), New York: Hafner Publishing Company, 1951. (First published in German in 1790)

Kant, Immanuel, *Observations on the Feeling of the Beautiful and Sublime* (trans. John T. Goldthwait), Berkeley: University of California Press, 1960 (First published in German in 1764)

Kass, Thomas, 'Morbid Melancholy, the Imagination and Samuel Johnson's Sermons', *Logos: A Journal of Catholic Thought and Culture.* 8(4):47-63. 2005

Kierkegaard, Søren, *Either/Or: A Fragment of Life* (trans. Alistair Hannay), London: Penguin, 1992 (First published 1843)

Klibansky, Raymond, Erwin Panofsky and Fritz Saxl, *Saturn and Melancholy: Studies in the History of Natural Philosophy, Religion and Art*, London: Thomas Nelson and Sons, 1964

Kristeva, Julia, *Black Sun: Depression and Melancholia*, New York: Columbia University Press, 1989

Landis, Olaf Blanke Theodor, 'The Metaphysical Art of Giorgio de Chirico: Migraine or Epilepsy?', *European Neurology*, 50: 191-194. 2003

Lange, Susanne, *Bernd and Hilla Becher: Life and Work* (trans. Jeremy Gaines), Boston: MIT Press, 2006

Larson, Kent, *Louis I. Kahn: Unbuilt Masterworks*, New York: The Monacelli Press, 2000

Lévi-Strauss, Claude, *Tristes Tropiques* (trans. John and Dorreen Weightman), London: Jonathan Cape, 1973 (First published 1955 by Librairie Plon)

Lichtenstein, Rachel and Iain Sinclair, *Rodinsky's Room*, London: Granta Books, 2000

Lorca, Federico García, *In Search of Duende* (trans. Christopher Maurer, JL Gili, Norman Thomas Di Giovanni), New York: New Directions, 1998

Lorris, Guillaume de and Jean de Meun, *The Romance of the Rose* (trans. Charles Dahlberg), Princeton: Princeton University Press, 1995

Lowenthal, David, *The Past is a Foreign Country.* Cambridge: Cambridge University Press, 1985

Lowes, John Livingston, 'The Loveres Maladye of Hereos', *Modern Philology*, 11,(4): 491-546. 1914

Lowrie, Walter, *Kierkegaard*, New York: Harper, 1962

Marin, Louis, *Sublime Poussin* (trans. Catherine Porter), Palo Alto CA: Stanford University Press, 1999

Marion, Jean-Luc, *God Without Being*, Chicago: University of Chicago Press, 1991

Mark, Christopher, 'Messiaen: 'Quatuor pour la fin du temps' by Anthony Pople'. *Music & Letters,* 82(1): 143–145, p.144. 2001

Marker, Chris, *Immemory*, (CD ROM) Cambridge, MA: Exact Change, 2002

Martin, Wendy, *The Cambridge Introduction to Emily Dickinson*, Cambridge: Cambridge University Press, 2007

Mas, Antonio Contreras, '*Libro de la Melancholía* by Andrés Velázquez (1585). Part 1. The intellectual origins of the book', *History of Psychiatry*, 14(1): 25–40. 2003

Maurer, Naomi E, *The Pursuit of Spiritual Wisdom: The Thought and Art of Vincent Van Gogh*, Vancouver: Fairleigh Dickinson University Press, 1998

McDermott, John F, 'Emily Dickinson Revisited: A Study of Periodicity in Her Work', *American Journal of Psychiatry*, 158:686–690. 2001

Mellers, Wilfrid Howard, *Celestial Music?: Some Masterpieces of European Religious Music*, Woodbridge, Suffolk: Boydell and Brewer, 2002

Michelis, Marco de and Robert Fitzpatrick, *Hiroshi Sugimoto: Architecture*, Chicago: DAP Museum of Contemporary Art, 2003

Montaigne, Michel de, *The Complete Essays* (trans. MA Screech), London: Penguin, 1993

Montandon, Mark, *Innocent When You Dream: The Tom Waits Reader*, New York: Thunder's Mouth Press, 2005

Moody, Ivan, 'Giya Kancheli: An Introduction to His Music', *Tempo*, New Series, No. 173, Soviet Issue: 49–52. 1990

Moore, Thomas, *The Care of the Soul,* New York: Harper Collins, 1996

Morris, Marla, *Curriculum and the Holocaust: Competing Sites of Memory and Representation*, Mahwah, NJ: Lawrence Erlbaum Associates, 2001

Neill, Sam and Judy Rymer, *Cinema of Unease: A Personal Journey*, Video, British Film Institute, 1995

Nygren, Edward J, *Views and Visions: American Landscapes before 1830*, Washington DC: Corcoran Gallery of Art, 1986

O'Brien, Kerry, 'Mime Artist Bows Out', Australian Broadcasting

Corporation, 2007. Available at http://www.abc.net.au/7.30/content/2007/s2041546.htm

Pallasmaa, Juhani, 'Identity, Domicile and Identity: Notes on the Phenomenology of Home', From *The Concept of Home: An Interdiciplinary View* – symposium at the University of Trondheim, Norway, 21-23 August 1992, available at http://www2.uiah.fi/esittely/historia/e_ident.htm

Pamuk, Orhan, *Istanbul: Memories of a City* (trans. Maureen Freely), London: Faber and Faber, 2005

Panofsky, Erwin, *Meaning in the Visual Arts*, Chicago: University of Chicago Press, 1993

Pareles, Jon ,'Melancholy Melodies in Armenian Tradition', *New York Times,* January 15 1994

Parker, Gordon, 'The DSM Classification of Depressive Disorders: Debating Its Utility', *The Canadian Journal of Psychiatry*, 51(14): 871-873. 1996

Paton, Justin, 'Living Proof', in Laurence Aberhart, *Aberhart*, Wellington: Victoria University Press, 2007

Porter, Roy, 'Introduction' in George Cheyne, *The English Malady*, London, Routledge, 1991. (First published 1733)

Pushkin, Aleksandr Sergeevich, *Eugene Onegin*, Princeton: Princeton University Press, 1991. (First published 1833)

Putney, Christopher R, 'Acedia and the *Daemonium Meridianum* in Nikolaj Gogol's 'Povest'o tom, kak possorilsja Ivan Ivanovič s Ivanom Nikiforovičem', *Russian Literature* XLIX (2001) 235-257, 2001

Radden, Jennifer, *The Nature of Melancholy: From Aristotle to Kristeva*, New York: Oxford University Press, 2000

Ramalho, Maria Irene, Sousa Santos, Irene Ramalho Santos, *Atlantic Poets: Fernando Pessoa's Turn in Anglo-American Modernism*, Hanover: The University Press of New England, 2003

Renner, Rolf Günter, *Edward Hopper, 1882-1967: Transformation of the Real* Köln: Taschen, 2000

Reynolds, Ann, *Robert Smithson: Learning from New Jersey and Elsewhere*, Boston: MIT Press, 2002

Riding, Alan, 'An Artist sets up House(s) at the Grand Palais', *The New York Times*, May 31 2007

Roberts, W Wright, 'The Problem of Satie', *Music & Letters*, 4(4): 313–320. 1923

Rodenbach, Georges, *Bruges-la-Morte* (trans. Philip Mosley), Chicago: University of Scranton Press, 2007 (First published 1892)

Ross, Christine, *The Aesthetics of Disengagement: Contemporary Art and Depression*, Minneapolis: University of Minnesota Press, 2006

Ruff, Thomas and Matthias Winzen, *Thomas Ruff: Photography 1979 to the Present*, New York: DAP, 2003

Sadlier, Darlene J, *An Introduction to Fernando Pessoa: Modernism and the Paradoxes of Authorship*, Gainesville: University of Florida Press, 1998

Sagan, Françoise, *Bonjour Tristesse* (trans. Irene Ash), London, Penguin Books, 2007 (First published 1954 by Rene Juilliard)

Sánchez-Pardo, Esther, *Cultures of the Death Drive: Melanie Klein and Modernist Melancholia*, Durham: Duke University Press, 2003

Santner, Eric L, *Stranded Objects: Mourning, Memory and Film in Postwar Germany*, Ithaca, NY: Cornell University Press, 1990

Sarafianos, Aris, 'The many colours of black bile: the melancholies of knowing and feeling', *Papers of Surrealism*, 4: 1–17, 2005

Sartre, Jean-Paul, *Nausea* (trans. Robert Baldick), Harmondsworth: Penguin Books, 1965 (First published as *La Nausée* in 1938)

Schwenger, Peter, *The Tears of Things: Melancholy and Physical Objects*, Minneapolis: University of Minnesota Press, 2006

Screech, Michael Andrew and Marc Fumaroli, *Montaigne and Melancholy: The Wisdom of the Essays*, Lanham, MD: Rowman and Littlefield, 2000

Sebald, WG, *The Emigrants* (trans. Michael Hulse), New York: New Directions, 1996 (First published as *Die Ausgewanderten* 1992)

Sebald, WG, *The Rings of Saturn* (trans. Michael Hulse), New York: New Directions Books, 1998 (First published in German as *Die Ringe des Saturn, Eine englische Wallfahrt*, 1995)

Sebald, WG, *Vertigo* (trans. Michael Hulse), New York: New Directions, 1999. (First published as *Schwindel. Gefuhle* 1990)

Shakespeare, William, *Four Comedies ('As You Like It')*, London: Penguin Books, 1994

Shakespeare, William, *Hamlet*, Cambridge: Cambridge University Press, 1999

Shakespeare, William, *Twelfth Night, or What You Will*, New York: Dover Publications, 1999 (First published c.1623)

Shelley, Percy Bysshe, 'Alastor: Or, the Spirit of Solitude' in *The Major Works*, Oxford: Oxford University Press, 2003

Shklovlsky, Victor, 'Art as Technique', in Lee T. Lemon and Marion J. Reis (Trans.), *Russian Formalist Criticism: Four Essays*. Lincoln: University of Nebraska Press, 1965 (Original essay published 1917)

Siegel, Linda, 'Synaesthesia and the Paintings of Caspar David Friedrich', *Art Journal*, 33(3): 196-204. 1974

Sinclair, Iain, *Lights out for the Territory: 9 Excursions in the Secret History of London*, London: Granta Books,1997

Sinclair, Iain, *London: City of Disappearances*, London: Hamish Hamilton, 2006

Smith, Allan, 'Romanticist and Symbolist Tendencies in Recent New Zealand Photography', *Art New Zealand*, 64: 80-84, and 111. 1992

Smith, Bernard H, *European Vision and the South Pacific* (2nd edition), Sydney: Harper and Row, 1985

Smith, Geoff, 'An Interview with Arvo Pärt: Sources of Invention', *The Musical Times*, 140(1868): 19-22 and 24-25. 1999

Smithson, Robert, 'The Monuments of Passaic', *ArtForum*, 6(4), 48-51. 1967

Solà-Morales Rubió, Ignasi de, 'Terrain Vague' in Cynthia Davidson (ed), *Anyplace*, Boston: MIT Press,1995

Sontag, Susan, *Against Interpretation, and Other Essays*, New York: Farrar, Straus and Giroux, 1996

Sontag, Susan, *Illness as Metaphor and AIDS and its Metaphors*, New York: Picador, 2001

Sontag, Susan, *Regarding the Pain of Others*, New York: Farrar, Straus and Giroux, 2003

Sontag, Susan, *The Volcano Lover*, London: Vintage, 1993

Sontag, Susan, *Under the Sign of Saturn*, New York: Picador, 2002

Starobinski, Jean, *The Invention of Liberty, 1700-1789*, New York: Rizzoli, 1987

Stendhal, *Love.* (trans. Gilbert and Suzanne Sale), London: Penguin, 1975 (First published 1822)

Stewart, Susan, 'Garden Agon', *Representations*, No. 62. (Spring, 1998), pp.111-143

Straub, Jürgen, *Narration, Identity and Historical Consciousness*, New York: Berghahn Books, 2005

Strong, Roy, *The Renaissance Garden in England*, London: Thames and Hudson, 1998

Sunday Star Times Magazine, 29 January 2006, 17

Svensden, Lars, *A Philosophy of Boredom* (trans. John Irons), London: Reaktion Books, 2005

Swan, Claudia, *Art, Science and Witchcraft in Early Modern Holland*, Cambridge: Cambridge University Press, 2005

Toohey, Peter and Kathleen Toohey, 'Giorgio de Chirico, Time, Odysseus, Melancholy, and Intestinal Disorder', in Peter Toohey, *Melancholy, Love, and Time*, Ann Arbor: University of Michigan Press, 2004

Tosatto, Guy, 'The Time of Photography', in Thomas Struth, *Still*, New York: The Monacelli Press, 2001

Trevor, Douglas (2004). *The Poetics of Melancholy in Early Modern Europe*, Cambridge: Cambridge University Press.

Trigg, Dylan, *The Aesthetics of Decay: Nothingness, Nostalgia and the Absence of Reason*, New York: Peter Lang, 2006

Trigg, Dylan, 'Schopenhauer and the Sublime Pleasure of Tragedy', *Philosophy and Literature*, 28(1): 165–179, p.168. 2004

Tupper, Frederick, 'Ubi sunt: A Belated Postscript', *Modern Language Notes*, 28(6): 197-198. 1913

Vasari, Giorgio, *The Lives of the Artists* (trans. George Bull), Harmondsworth: Penguin Books, 1965 (First published 1568)

Vaz, Katherine, *Saudade*, New York: St Martin's Press, 1994

Viatte, Germain, 'Passages', in *Dani Karavan: Passages – Homage to Walter Benjamin*, Tel Aviv: Tel Aviv Museum of Art, 1998

Vidler, Anthony, *The Architectural Uncanny: Essays in the Modern Unhomely*, Boston: MIT Press, 1992

Virgil, *Virgil: Eclogues. Georgics. Aeneid 1-6* (trans. H. Rushton Fairclough), Boston: Harvard University Press, 1986

Von Rezzori, Gregor, *Memoirs of an anti-Semite*. New York, Viking Press, 1981

Waits, Tom, *Alice*, Epitaph Records, released in 2002

Waits, Tom, *Nighthawks at the Diner*, Asylum Records, 1975

Wannan, Bill, *The Australian: Yarns, Ballads, Legends, Traditions of the*

Australian People, Adelaide: Rigby, 1963

Wierzbicka, Anna, *Emotions Across Languages and Cultures: Diversity and Universals*, Cambridge: Cambridge University Press, 1999

Wilkins, Richard, 'Cultural Frames: Loci of intercultural communication asynchrony in a CBS 60 Minutes news segment', *International Journal of Intercultural Relations* 31(2): 243–258, 2006

Williamson, George, 'Mutability, Decay, and Seventeenth-Century Melancholy', *ELH*, 2(2): 121–150. 1935

Wilson, Janelle L, *Nostalgia: Sanctuary of Meaning,* Lewisburg, PA: Bucknell University Press, 2005

Wittkower, Rudolf and Margot, *Born Under Saturn: The Character and Conduct of Artists: A Documented History from Antiquity to the French Revolution*, New York: Random House, 1963

Woodward, Christopher, *In Ruins*, London: Vintage, 2001

Yates, Frances, *The Art of Memory*, Chicago: University of Chicago Press, 1974. (First published 1966)

Yates, Frances A, *The Occult Philosophy in the Elizabethan Age*, London: Routledge and Kegan Paul, 1979

Ye, Zhengdao, 'An inquiry into sadness in Chinese', in Jean Harkins and Anna Wierzbicka (eds), *Emotions in crosslinguistic perspective*, Berlin: Mouton de Gruyter, 2001

Yeats, William Butler, *Letters to Katharine Tynan*, New York: McMullen Books, 1953

Zimmerman, Johann Georg (1796) *Solitude Considered*, cited in Wolf Lepenies *Melancholy and Society* (trans Jeremy Gaines and Doris Jones), Cambridge, MA: Harvard University Press, 1992

Žižek, Slavoj, *Did Somebody say Totalitarianism? Five Interventions on the (Mis)use of a Notion*, London: Verso, 2001

Žižek, Slavoj, 'Melancholy and the Critical Act', *Critical Inquiry* 26(4): 657–681. 2000

Index